COOL
ENTERTAINING

COOL ENTERTAINING

Irma Rhode

Introduction by James Beard

NEW YORK

Atheneum

1976

Library of Congress Cataloging in Publication Data
Main entry under title: Cool entertaining
1. Cookery (Cold dishes) 2. Buffets (Cookery)
I. Rhode, Irma, 1900–
TX830.C66   1976   641.7'9   75–41420
ISBN 0–689–10710–2

Designed by Kathleen Carey
First Edition

INTRODUCTION

James Beard

I'VE KNOWN Irma Rhode for almost forty years. The day we met was very significant for me; in fact it changed my life completely. I had been invited to a cocktail party to meet Irma and her brother Bill at a time when I was looking for an idea to get into the food business, as were they. We discovered we were kindred spirits, and planned and finally opened our late-lamented shop, which we called Hors d'oeuvre Incorporated. Irma not only knew food, she had great scientific ability. Bill understood good living and had enough charm to win anyone's heart. I had ambition and a knowledge of food—and personality. The three of us made a bold move and opened on East 66th Street, right next to the Cosmopolitan Club. It was a success! When war came we were forced to close: Bill Rhode went on to be one of the first editors of Gourmet magazine, I went to the wars and Irma did a great variety of things and our paths never crossed professionally again.

Despite Bill's death Irma and I have continued a warm and lasting friendship. Her enthusiasm, her delight in entertaining and her vast knowledge of food and drink have given Irma a full, rich life. She is always bubbling. I have seldom seen her down; her sense of humor is a perpetual delight.

This latest volume of hers is a very personal book; it's filled with Irma. There are recipes for a variety of cold dishes—a great many of which I have enjoyed in Irma's home. It's a book for good entertaining —one that will be in the front line of my collection of cookbooks.

PREFACE

TO BE PREPARED is everything, be it war or peace, love or entertaining. I love to give parties, and I have given many, from small, intimate dinners at home to affairs for a large number of people, in my professional life. And I have learned one thing from all of them. Plan and prepare ahead, otherwise the party is a dud and you are a nervous wreck.

There were parties given in the department store where I was once food director. Requests from the buyers' offices for Danish and sandwiches were easy to fulfill; harder were the requests for cold roast turkey with stuffing and all the trimmings from the maintenance department. They always occurred during the holiday season, or during special sales, when the cafeteria was busier than usual. It takes a great deal of planning to give a party the day before Christmas, even if you have large commercial ovens and roasting pans that hold two 25-pound turkeys. Of course, the store was open late at night so that gave us time.

Larger, far larger, were the annual open-house parties for the old-age home in a castle on the banks of the Harlem River. The old building had a high ground floor used for the residents' recreational activities where we had the cocktail parties, often for more than 500 people. Planning started six weeks before the event, usually on a Monday in May. Every detail was carefully checked and the timing worked out so the residents could be served supper while the cocktail party was going on. When the residents were finished the dining room was reset for the buffet supper offered to the cocktail party guests lingering at the bar. We made thousands of hors d'oeuvres; you will find the recipes for these in the first chapter of this book. The chefs deviled a crate of eggs—that's thirty dozen—and even the residents helped with the onion rings. The timetable called for a start on Friday night. A basket of parsley was washed and plucked, then wrapped up to be chopped the next day. The spreads needed were mixed so that on Saturday all the hors d'oeuvres that had to be prechilled could be made up. Also, everything that had to be sliced was prepared so that on Sunday the great assembly could start. The finished hors d'oeuvres were stored in the iceboxes and the chefs began roasting and baking the meats for the buffet and preparing the salads to be put in bowls for garnishing on Monday. While the residents had their Sunday supper all my volunteers and I set up the bar in the recreation room.

Premixing drinks is great fun. We took large stockpots and poured bottle after bottle of gin and whiskey in the agreed proportions for the martinis and Manhattans. After stirring gently with large paddles, the mixtures were poured back into the bottles with the help of funnels and small ladles. Then they were distributed to the four bar stations, other bottles were opened, glasses were set up and by eight o'clock the bar was ready to go. By that time the kitchen was empty and we began arranging the hors d'oeuvres on large silver platters rented from a catering supply house. By midnight Sunday, all trays were stored in the walk-in iceboxes ready to go at 5:30 P.M. on Monday. That's how I know the hors d'oeuvres keep.

On Monday I turned stage manager, rehearsing the waitresses, explaining to them in detail what they had to do. The timing was always critical in setting up the dining room after the residents' supper. We checked the rented tablecloths for holes or other defects and we always ordered extra, just to be insured against that calamity.

In all the years there were only two near misses. One year the iceman was late, arriving just five minutes before the bar was to be opened, and another year we ran out of coffee, but fortunately the hot water urn was still going, so it took only a few minutes to make another five gallons of coffee.

As much fun as these parties were, they were also a lot of work and I was glad when the moment arrived when I could take off my shoes and leave the cleaning to others.

My private parties, usually for six or eight guests, are of course on a much smaller scale. But even for these I write the menu on the left side of a piece of paper and the shopping list for each course on the right side and make a timetable. Just thinking through a party is a great help. It also helps to know one's limitations, face them, and work around them.

My kitchen is a glorified closet and the dining area seats eight or nine with no room to spare. Therefore, I have a bar set up in the living room, eliminating the need to go into the kitchen to fix drinks. Also, instead of serving first courses at the table, I prepare lots of hors d'oeuvres and call them a first course, thus reducing the number of dishes to be washed and keeping the scarce counterspace free.

Depending on the menus, the timetable may call for preparations to start on Tuesday for a Friday dinner. But by Thursday night all is ready. While my guests are having cocktails, about ten or fifteen minutes before serving time, I slice the meat, put salads in bowls and unmold aspics and desserts. It depends on the size of the group whether I set up a buffet on a separate table or have double service —small bowls and platters placed on both ends of the dining room table—and at other times I do all the serving from a cart.

Salads that can be prepared in advance are ideal. Rarely are green salads on my menu, since they are such usual fare, requiring extra dishes and last minute fixings, and keeping me in the kitchen while my guests are in the living room.

It may seem strange to start cooking on Tuesday for a Friday dinner but actually it's timesaving. One has to be in the kitchen anyway to cook the day's dinner, so why not put another roast in the oven and cook extra potatoes, rice or vegetables to use for salads. Once you get the knack of this, your cold dishes can be ready without spending extra time in the kitchen.

Cold suppers were the custom as long as the main hot meal was served at noon. They had one great advantage: all the cooking was done in the morning and the afternoons were free for other activities. The famous Kaffeeklatches—the housewives' get-togethers—were held around four o'clock; all the women were secure in the knowledge that the evening meal was ready to be served and that there were no pots and pans to be washed that night.

Europeans, especially northern Europeans, still serve cold suppers, because most places of business serve hot noon meals. The mothers and children have their hot meals around noon, when the children come home from school. It is a relief not to have to start cooking again in the afternoon and messing up the kitchen.

I often wonder whether this culinary timetable, this clinging to the old routine, has something to do with the short summers in northern Europe, when time is too precious to waste in the kitchen, or whether it is just an inborn efficiency drive. Whatever it may be, the cold supper habit persists in Europe for all intimate entertaining. Of course Europeans do give elaborate dinner parties, from soup to nuts, but only for special occasions. The food industry complements this cold supper custom and there are delicatessens throughout Europe unlike any found even in New York. If you have the money, you don't have to cook. It's all there, from fresh caviar and truffled paté to just plain potato salad.

But planning is still necessary. All these stores close early in accordance with union rules, so there cannot be too much last minute shopping or maybe getting an impromptu, spur of the moment party together. There are plans for these, too, so you don't have to keep your guests waiting for hours for chickens and other frozen foods to defrost. Just be prepared for everything.

You may wonder why there are so many recipes in this book requiring "plain gelatin." Hot foods are held together by various sauces; cold foods by gelatin solutions that are liquid while warm and solid when cold; mayonnaise, a blend of oil and egg yolks; or its cousin, a sort of cold Hollandaise, made with melted butter and egg yolks. The binder may be a combination of gelatin solution and mayonnaise or a white sauce made with gelatinous stock, usually chicken or veal. This is the "Chaudfroid" of the classic cuisine, more or less solid when cold, the best example being cold chicken fricassee. Or the binder may be sour cream, either plain or seasoned.

Of all these various binders the gelatin solution is the only one free of fat, egg yolks and carbohydrates, and high in protein. I emphasize the gelatin solution, not necessarily the ingredients bound by the gelatin solution. Therefore, a gelatin-solution binder is the one that meets closest the trends of modern nutrition.

But don't think for a minute that gelatin dishes are a modern invention, beginning when commercial gelatin became available. The old chefs were adept at creating many gelatin dishes, only they derived the gelatin from boiling the bones of animal feet and knuckles. Remember the famous remedy "calf's foot jelly," so highly prized in the sickrooms? Chicken feet, of course, properly scrubbed and pedicured, were an ideal source of gelatin, and there was not a chicken soup made without chicken feet. Where does one get chicken feet today, except in special shops such as kosher butchers? We just have to rely on little bags of plain gelatin.

Another advantage of gelatin dishes is the fact that a gelatin solution will liquify when reheated. So it's easy to remold leftovers from a gelatin dish to make it look like new.

Salads, too, can be refreshed. If you wish to combine two leftover salads and feel that their dressings clash, put them in a colander, run hot water over them, shake them dry, chill and apply a new dressing. All this comes in handy around holiday time when one party follows the other. Perhaps you had a buffet party and want to use the leftovers to look freshly prepared for another, smaller party.

Even leftover whipped cream dishes can be reconstructed. Make a small amount of gelatin solution suitable to the leftover, chill it to egg white consistency, then whip it and gradually add the leftover whipped cream mixture. Pour into a mold or bowl and defy your guests to spot the leftover.

After more than forty years in the United States, I still entertain "European-style," offering different and interesting fare to my many American friends. After I retired, they asked me to write down all my cold supper recipes.

So here they are.

Irma Rhode
New York City

CONTENTS

CONTENTS

COOL
ENTERTAINING

HORS D'OEUVRES

ALL THE HORS D'OEUVRES described in the following chapter can be made the day before a large party. Make them up, chill, and store them in the vegetable bin of the refrigerator, where they will be ready to be put on platters as needed.

I have given up on hot hors d'oeuvres, as I cannot afford the luxury of somebody in the kitchen. They need a hot oven and split-second timing and I always burn them, being chief cook and bottle washer, bartender and hostess. But I always have a good cheese tray and experiment with new ones, to the delight of my friends. I often cut Swiss cheese into cubes, stick them with toothpicks and arrange them around a small dish of plain mustard. Or, do as my friend Sara Pride does, and fasten a small piece of crystallized ginger to a cube of Gouda cheese. But whatever you do, bring those cheeses out before getting dressed for the party. Cheeses need to be at room temperature to develop their flavor.

HAM AND PICKLE ROLLS

4 slices boiled ham, thinly sliced
12 very small gherkins
A little paprika in a saucer, or some chopped parsley

Cut ham into 12 strips about 1 inch wide and 1¾ inches long. Place a gherkin on one end, roll up and secure with a toothpick. Trim off ends and dip into parsley or paprika. If very small gherkins are not available, quarter larger ones. Instead of ham, corned beef may be used.

12 PIECES

HAM AND CHEESE ROLLS

6 slices boiled ham
6 sticks of cheese, about ¼ inch thick and ¼ inch wide
2 tablespoons butter
1 teaspoon prepared mustard

Any type of cheese may be used: American, Swiss, Muenster or Cheddar. If the cheese selected is of the pasteurized variety, use two or three slices pressed together, then cut into sticks.

Arrange ham slices on waxed paper, blend mustard and softened butter and spread on ham slices. Roll a cheese stick into the ham slice. Wrap each ham and cheese roll into a piece of waxed paper. Chill for at least 12 hours. Before serving, cut into cubes as desired and secure with a toothpick.

24 PIECES

ROAST BEEF ROLLS

3–4 slices thin roast beef, preferably rare
1 teaspoon dry mustard
1 tablespoon currant jelly
Chopped parsley

Arrange roast beef slices on a wooden board; do not trim off fat. Mix mustard and currant jelly and spread over roast beef slices. Roll them up rather tightly and cut into small rolls, about ¾ inch long, trimming off the ends. Secure with toothpick and dip each end into chopped parsley. Cover and chill.

12–14 PIECES

SALMON ROLLS

6 slices smoked salmon
2 tablespoons cream cheese, soft-
ened to room temperature

2 teaspoons prepared horseradish,
pressed dry, or use moist-
ened instant horseradish
Paprika

Arrange salmon slices on waxed paper and smooth them out. Mix cream cheese with horseradish and spread over salmon slices. Roll up. With a sharp knife cut each roll in half; trim the other ends and secure with toothpicks. Dip each end into paprika. Chill well before serving.

12 PIECES

CHERRY TOMATO CUPS

12 cherry tomatoes, not too small
6 ounces cream cheese
2 teaspoons chives, fresh or frozen
¼ teaspoon salt, or to taste

Cut off bottom end of tomatoes and stand on blossom end. With a small spoon scoop out the pulp and stand the tomatoes upside down to drain. Blend softened cream cheese with chives and salt; season to taste.

When using frozen chives, do not defrost; this will prevent loss of flavor. Place cream cheese mixture into a pastry bag or cake decorator and fill the tomato cups. Chill well before serving.

12 PIECES

ARTICHOKE CUPS

12 artichoke hearts, canned, pref-
erably small
¾ cup chopped ham
1–1½ tablespoons mayonnaise

1 teaspoon finely chopped dill
pickles or gherkins
1 teaspoon chopped parsley

Drain artichokes, turning them upside down to drain off liquid between leaves. Trim off bottom point so they will stand straight. Press center leaves down gently to form a shallow cup. A thimble is very helpful.

Mix ham with 1 tablespoon mayonnaise, add the chopped pickles and only add more mayonnaise as needed, depending on moisture in the pickles. Fill artichokes with the ham mixture, making a small mound on top. Chill well before serving.

12 PIECES

ZUCCHINI CUPS WITH CRABMEAT

2 *baby zucchinis*
6 *ounces crabmeat, fresh, frozen*
    or canned
½ *teaspoon lemon juice*

1 *teaspoon Durkee Famous Sauce*
1 *tablespoon mayonnaise*
Salt and pepper to taste

Scrub zucchinis. Drop them into boiling water; when water returns to boiling point, drain. Chill. Defrost frozen crabmeat and drain well. Drain canned crabmeat. Sprinkle with lemon juice and let stand.

Trim the ends of the chilled zucchinis and divide each into 6 slices about ½ inch thick. With a melon ball cutter scoop out center, leaving a bottom. Press drained crabmeat dry and crumble to shred. Add Famous Sauce, mayonnaise and season to taste. Fill cups with crabmeat mixture, mounding the top. Chill well before serving.

12 PIECES

CUCUMBER CUPS WITH SHRIMP

2 *small, narrow fresh cucumbers*
¾ *cup chopped cooked shrimp,*
    fresh or canned, drained
1 *teaspoon fresh chopped dill*

1 *teaspoon Durkee Famous Sauce*
1 *tablespoon mayonnaise*
½ *teaspoon lemon juice*
Salt and pepper to taste

Peel cucumbers; with the tines of a fork, flute them lengthwise, all around. Cut each cucumber into 6 slices, about ½–¾ inch thick. With a melon ball cutter scoop out center of slice, leaving a bottom. Mix shrimp, dill, Famous Sauce, mayonnaise and lemon juice and season to taste. Fill cucumber cup with shrimp mixture, piling into a mound. Chill well before serving.

12 PIECES

BEET CUPS WITH CREAM CHEESE

6–8 small canned beets
4 ounces cream cheese at room temperature
1 teaspoon grated onion
1 teaspoon chopped parsley

Drain beets well; pat dry with paper toweling. Cut each beet in half. Groove the cut side with a melon ball cutter and take a slice off the rounded side to let the beet shells stand level. Blend cream cheese, onions and parsley and place in a pastry bag. Fill the beet cups neatly, making a rosette on top.

Since they stain easily, store the beet cups in a flat bottomed trough made from aluminum foil.

12–16 PIECES

ONION CUPS WITH LIVERWURST

12 small canned onions   *⅛ pound liverwurst*
¾ cup pickling liquid (left from *½ tablespoon mayonnaise*
pickles or gherkins)   *1 teaspoon prepared mustard*

Drain onions and remove center using a small pickle fork. Bring pickling liquid to the boiling point. Pour over onion cups and let stand for 12 hours. Drain cups and pat dry with paper toweling. Blend liverwurst, mayonnaise and mustard. Using a very small knife, fill onion cups. Chill well before serving.

12 PIECES

PENNY RADISHES

12 slices raw carrots, about ¼ inch thick	Salt
	12 radishes
1 tablespoon butter at room temperature	*12 fancy toothpicks*

Spread carrot slices with butter and salt them lightly. Cut radish slices from the leaf ends. Trim the root end and insert a toothpick. Place the radishes cut side down on the carrot slices and press the toothpicks down far enough to secure the carrot slices, but not to penetrate them. Chill before serving.

These make an excellent garnish for all sorts of cold platters, not only hors d'oeuvres.

12 PIECES

HEARTS OF PALM WITH ROQUEFORT CHEESE SPREAD

1 can hearts of palm, well chilled	*2 ounces (½ stick) butter at room temperature*
4 ounces Roquefort cheese at room temperature	*1 teaspoon whiskey*
	Ground nutmeg

Drain hearts of palm and pat them dry with paper toweling. Cut into rounds about ½–¾ inch thick. Blend Roquefort cheese, butter and whiskey and place in a pastry tube. Top each heart of palm round with a neat rosette of the Roquefort cheese spread. Dust very lightly with ground nutmeg. Chill well before serving.

12–18 PIECES

CHEESE AND HAM CUBES

1 can deviled ham spread (2–3 ounces)
¼ teaspoon prepared mustard
1 teaspoon butter
4 slices cheese, American, Swiss or Muenster

Soften butter and mix with deviled ham and mustard. Spread one slice of cheese with ham mixture and place second slice of cheese on top. Repeat until all slices of cheese have been used. Wrap tightly in waxed paper and chill for at least 6 hours. Cut into cubes before serving.

9–12 PIECES

SALAMI CORNUCOPIAS

6 slices salami
4 ounces cream cheese at room temperature
1–2 teaspoons chopped chives
¼ teaspoon salt

Cut salami slices in half. Twist each half into a cornucopia and insert into a square of a cake rack, or use the baskets with square lattice used for produce.

Mix cream cheese, chives and salt. If using frozen chives, do not defrost. Using a pastry bag, fill the cornucopias. Press the edges slightly against the filling so as to secure the open end. If needed, add a bit of cream cheese to the top flap. Chill until cream cheese is set, then remove from basket and arrange on a plate. Cover lightly; chill overnight. If desired, use only 3 ounces of cream cheese and 1 ounce butter.

12 PIECES

DEVILED EGGS WITHOUT MAYONNAISE

6 eggs, hard cooked and peeled
¾ cup chicken stock, canned or
   homemade
2 teaspoons unflavored gelatin

1 teaspoon prepared mustard
1 teaspoon chopped parsley
½ teaspoon salt
½ teaspoon Worcestershire sauce

Cut eggs in half through the middle, remove yolks and cut off tip to make a straight standing cup. The broader end of the egg half usually does not require leveling. Press yolks through a sieve.

Heat chicken stock to the boiling point; add gelatin and stir to dissolve. Reheat a bit if necessary. Add mustard, parsley, salt and Worcestershire sauce. Chill until it begins to jell. Beat lightly, then add egg yolks. The mixture should now be just right for pressing through a pastry tube. If not, let stand until a bit firmer.

Fill egg cups with mixture using the pastry tube. Let chill, then cover lightly with waxed paper. These deviled eggs, without mayonnaise, will keep better and tend to be less dried out after a night's chilling.

12 PIECES

MOCK PETITS FOURS
from Pumpernickel

3 slices darkest pumpernickel
6 ounces Cheddar cheese spread at room temperature
2 ounces (½ stick) butter at room temperature

Combine cheese spread and butter, blending very well. Spread two slices of the pumpernickel heavily with the cheese–butter mixture. Place the third slice of bread on top, triple-decker fashion. Wrap in waxed paper and chill until set.

Put the remaining cheese mixture into a pastry bag. Cut the well chilled triple decker sandwich into 12 squares. With the pastry bag top each square with a dab of the cheese mixture, making a rosette or other decorative design. Chill well before serving.

12 PIECES

MOCK PETITS FOURS
from Ham and Cheese

3 slices boiled ham
2 slices Swiss cheese (any other
    cheese about the size of a
    ham slice may be used)

1 tablespoon butter
½ teaspoon prepared mustard

COATING:

½ cup chicken or beef broth
1 teaspoon plain gelatin
1 teaspoon mayonnaise
9 or 12 capers

Soften butter and blend with mustard. Spread over a slice of ham; top with a slice of cheese. Spread cheese slice with butter and top with a slice of ham. Repeat with second slice of cheese and then top with a slice of ham. Wrap in waxed paper and chill.

To prepare the coating, sprinkle ½ cup broth with gelatin, heat and stir to dissolve, cool. Add mayonnaise. Set in a pan of ice cubes and stir gently every once in a while till it has the consistency of heavy syrup.

Cut ham and cheese package into 9 or 12 cubes as desired. Spear each cube with a toothpick. Dip into the syrup and place on a tray or other flat surface. Chill. When set, remove toothpick and place a caper on the spot.

9–12 PIECES

ONION RINGS

Onion rings are one of the most popular hors d'oeuvres. The following recipe has been written up many times and is listed in the *New York Times Cook Book* as "Irma's Onion Sandwiches," but I cannot claim credit. The true story of the evolution of this recipe is as follows: In the twenties, in a Parisian establishment described by Polly Adler as "a house that's not a home," two slices of leftover breakfast brioches, spread with mayonnaise and filled with a slice of onion, were served with the apéritifs to my brother Bill.

When in the thirties we started Hors d'Oeuvres Inc., he remembered the combination and we started testing. How thick the brioche slices, how thin the onion? What size cookie cutter? Two bites or a bite and a half? When my brother Bill, Jim Beard and I finally had decided on these questions, there arose another one. How to dress them up? There always was a big bowl of chopped parsley around and, of course, mayonnaise. I can still see Jim rolling the edges in mayonnaise and then in chopped parsley, and the new onion rings were born. But it all goes back to the thrifty madam of that establishment in Paris.

6 slices of firm white bread, on the sweet side, or use 12 slices of challah (Jewish bread used for Sabbath)

12 slices onion, very thin
Approximately ½ cup mayonnaise
Approximately ¾ cup very finely chopped parsley

With a 1½ inch cookie cutter, cut 4 rounds from a slice of bread or 2 rounds from the challah slices. Arrange them in 12 pairs. Spread each round with mayonnaise. Using either a slicer or a potato peeler, cut the slices of onions and put one on a bread round. Salt lightly, then top with the second round, sandwich fashion. When all 12 are assembled, spread some mayonnaise on a piece of waxed paper and have the chopped parsley ready in a bowl. Take a sandwich between thumb and forefinger and roll the edges first in the thinly spread mayonnaise, then in the chopped parsley. Make sure there are no bare spots; if so, dab a bit of mayonnaise on the spot and dip again in parsley. Place on waxed paper on a flat tray or cookie sheet and cover with waxed paper. Chill well.

Note: If it's too hard to get very thin slices of onions perfectly round, part slices will do, too; use two or more parts. The thinness is important.

12 PIECES

WATERCRESS ROLLS

12 slices of cooked smoked tongue or soft salami

2 tablespoons cream cheese at room temperature

1 teaspoon prepared horseradish, pressed dry, or use moistened instant horseradish

24 sprigs watercress, washed and drained

2 or 3 inch wide strips of waxed paper about 20 inches long

Lay out slices of tongue or salami. Mix cream cheese and horseradish; spread on slices, making sure that the mixture covers them well. Place a sprig of watercress on each side, then roll up in such a manner that the leaves of the cress are free. Press gently to secure.

After preparing 6 rolls, wrap them in one of the long strips of waxed paper, making sure that the leaves are covered and that the paper separates each roll. Unwrap just before serving. This will protect the cress leaves from wilting. Chill for at least 3–4 hours, or overnight.

12 PIECES

CHINESE ROLLS

6 slices of roast pork, thinly sliced
3 preserved kumquats with juice
Sesame seeds

Arrange slices of roast pork on a wooden board. Cut each in half, lengthwise. Quarter kumquats so as to have 12 longish sticks. Place one of the sticks at the end of each pork slice and roll up. Secure with toothpicks. Sprinkle sesame seeds on the board and pour the kumquat juice into a saucer. Trim the ends of the pork rolls, as needed. Then dip each end first in the kumquat juice, then in the sesame seeds. Cover and chill.

12 PIECES

DIP FOR LOBSTER CUBES

8–10 ounces frozen lobster tails
½ cup mayonnaise
½ cup yoghurt
1 teaspoon Durkee Famous Sauce

4 tablespoons finely chopped fresh dill (if using a blender leave dill sprigs whole)
Salt and pepper to taste

Cook lobster tails according to directions on package. Drain immediately. When cool enough to handle, split lobster tails in half through the back and remove meat. Cut into cubes and put toothpicks through cubes. Cover and chill. Combine mayonnaise, yoghurt, Durkee Famous Sauce and fresh dill. Chill. Serve dip in a bowl surrounded with lobster cubes.

For a dip with a heavier consistency: Blend ½ cup of cold milk with 1½ teaspoons cornstarch. Bring to the boiling point and simmer until thickened. Cool. Add to other ingredients and blend well.

12–18 PIECES

LOBSTER SPREAD

8 ounces shelled lobster tail,	*Salt and pepper to taste*
canned or cooked	*Mayonnaise, enough to make a*
2 teaspoons capers	*smooth spread*
½ teaspoon onion juice	

Mix lobster and capers, chop together coarsely. Season with salt and pepper and onion juice; add enough mayonnaise to bind. Place in bowl; spread top with mayonnaise. Cover with waxed paper and chill. Serve on toast, crackers or chips.

MAKES 1 CUP

ROQUEFORT SPREAD

This cheese spread keeps so well, it can be prepared in large quantities and is very opportune for unexpected guests.

2 parts blue cheese
1 part butter or margarine
Sherry

Moisten blue cheese with sherry, as needed. Mash and blend with butter. Put into covered crock or jar and chill. Will keep for 3 to 4 weeks.

FRESH ARTICHOKE CUPS

12 artichokes, small, or 3 to 6 larger ones (very small or baby artichokes are the best)	*1 onion* *½ bay leaf* *½ lemon, cut into pieces* *1 tablespoon salt*

Place artichokes in a pot, cover with water. Add onion, bay leaf, lemon and salt, bring to boil. Cook until artichokes are done. Small ones will cook in 8 to 10 minutes, medium in 15 to 20 minutes and large in about 25 minutes. To test whether cooked, take one artichoke from the water and try pulling out one of the inner leaves; if this comes out easily, the artichokes are done. Strip artichokes of all outer green leaves and peel until the lighter inner leaves appear. Cut straight across about ½ inch above the rim of the bottom. Pull out center leaves, leaving a ring of 4 to 6 inner leaves. With a melon cutter or small spoon scrape out the choke, which is hardly developed in the very small artichokes. Trim the bottom and cut a level foot. Fill with chicken spread. See spreads, page 16.

12 PIECES

CARROT CUPS

3–4 carrots, about 1–1½ inches thick on top *4 ounces cream cheese at room temperature* *1 teaspoon finely chopped black olives*	*2 teaspoons finely grated nuts: almonds, pecans or walnuts* *½ teaspoon salt, or to taste*

Scrape carrots and if desired cut off 4 inches from the top. Drop the top ends or the whole carrots into boiling water and simmer for 15–20 minutes until barely soft. Do not overcook or they will break. Drain and chill. To make the cups groove the top end of the carrot, then slice off about ½ inch. Repeat grooving and slicing off. This is easier than slicing the carrots and then grooving the slices.

Blend cream cheese, olives and nuts and add salt. Taste for seasoning. Place cream cheese mixture in pastry bag and fill the grooved rounds. Chill well before serving.

CHICKEN SPREAD

With Nuts

> *1 cup chicken, leftover or canned*
> *½ cup shelled nuts: walnuts, pecans or hazelnuts*
> *Salt and pepper*
> *Mayonnaise*

Put chicken and nuts through meat grinder. Season to taste. Add enough mayonnaise to have a soft, but not runny, spread.

With Olives

Proceed as above and use olives in place of nuts. Either green, ripe or stuffed olives can be used.

With Chutney

Proceed as above and use 5 teaspoons chutney instead of nuts. If desired, flavor further with curry powder. When spread is mixed, place in bowl and cover top with light coating of mayonnaise. Garnish, if desired, with finely chopped egg whites. Cover bowl tightly and chill. Serve with crackers, toast or chips. Will keep in refrigerator for 36 hours.

MAKES I CUP, PLUS

LIVERWURST SPREAD

4 ounces liverwurst (¼ pound)
1 tablespoon grated onion
½ teaspoon prepared mustard
Mayonnaise

Mash liverwurst with onion and mustard. Add just enough mayonnaise to make a soft spread. Place in bowl, coat with mayonnaise and press a piece of waxed paper firmly on the surface. Chill. Serve with crackers or toast. Will keep in refrigerator for 36 hours.

MAKES ½ CUP

LIVER SPREAD

½ pound liver, beef, calf's or   *Salt and pepper to taste*
chicken, or leftover fried   *2 tablespoons butter*
or broiled liver   *2 hard cooked eggs (chopped sep-*
1 onion chopped, or leftover fried   *arately, yolks and whites,*
onions, chopped   *or together)*
3 tablespoons fat or butter

Sauté liver and onions in fat; do not brown. Put through meat grinder; season to taste. Add butter and chopped eggs (yolks and whites or just whites). Blend well and chill. Cover top with waxed paper firmly pressed down on the paste. Serve on toast or crackers. Will keep in refrigerator for 36 hours.

MAKES 1–1½ CUPS

MEAT SPREAD

This one will take care of all sorts of scraps, picked from the bones of a roast or just leftovers.

8 ounces cooked meat, either beef, pork or veal (about 1 cup)
1 raw onion
1 teaspoon sweet relish
Salt and pepper
Mayonnaise

Grind meat and onion in meat grinder. Mix with relish; add salt and pepper to taste. Blend in just enough mayonnaise to make a smooth spread. Place in bowl and coat lightly with mayonnaise. Cover tightly with waxed paper and chill. Serve on crackers, toast or chips; garnish with watercress if desired.

MAKES 1 CUP

HAM SPREAD

8 ounces ham, boiled or baked (leftover scraps)
1 large dill pickle
Salt and pepper to taste
Mayonnaise

Put ham and dill pickle through meat grinder. Season to taste. Add enough mayonnaise to bind. (If dill pickle is juicy, this may be a runny spread.) Place in bowl, coat surface lightly with mayonnaise, and cover tightly with waxed paper. Chill. Serve with toast, crackers or chips. Will keep in refrigerator for 36 hours.

MAKES 1 CUP

POTTED BLUE CHEESE

½ pound blue cheese
½ cup port wine
4 tablespoons butter or margarine

Pinch of salt
Dash of cayenne
¼ teaspoon Worcestershire sauce

Mash all ingredients, then blend with an electric mixer. Pack in small crocks covered tightly with waxed paper. (If larger quantities are to be prepared and stored, seal surface with paraffin, as for jellies.) Serve on crackers. Will keep in refrigerator for 6 weeks.

MAKES 1 CUP

POTTED CHEESE

Use any process cheese for this spread.

½ pound cheese, American, Cheddar or any other
2 tablespoons margarine
¼ cup sherry

Pinch of salt
¼ teaspoon paprika
Pinch of cayenne

Put cheese through the meat grinder. Add other ingredients. Blend well with electric mixer until very smooth. Place in small crock and cover tightly. Serve on crackers. Will keep in refrigerator for 6 weeks.

MAKES 1 CUP

QUICKIE EGG SPREAD

Leftover eggs from breakfast will come in handy for this spread.

3 hard cooked eggs
1 can anchovy fillets (2 ounces)

Chop eggs lightly, empty can of anchovies with oil over eggs. Mash with a fork until well blended. Chill well before serving on crackers.

MAKES ½ CUP

SARDINE SPREAD

1 can boneless sardines
1 teaspoon prepared mustard
Juice of 1 lemon

Empty can of sardines with oil on a plate. Add mustard and lemon juice and mash. To sharpen further, add a dash of Worcestershire sauce. Place in bowl, cover tightly with waxed paper and chill. Serve on toast or crackers.

MAKES ½ CUP

CLAM SPREAD

1 small can minced clams
Juice of 1 lemon
1 package cream cheese (3 to 4 ounces)
½ teaspoon grated onion
Bit of grated garlic
Pinch of powdered nutmeg
Pinch of powdered cloves
2 teaspoons mayonnaise, approximately

Drain clams well. Mix with lemon juice. Mash cheese; add onion, garlic and seasonings. Add clam mixture and mayonnaise to cheese (enough to make a soft spread). Place in bowl, cover tightly and chill. Serve with potato chips.

MAKES ¾ CUP

TURNIP CUPS

2–3 white young turnips, about 2½–3 inches in diameter
4 ounces cream cheese at room temperature
½ teaspoon celery salt
12 pecan halves

Peel turnips and slice into ½–¾ inch thick rounds. Cut each slice into 4 wedges. With a melon ball cutter, groove each wedge. Blend cream cheese and celery salt and put into a pastry bag. Fill the grooved wedges. Top the cream cheese with a pecan half.

12 PIECES

HAM AND CHEESE CUPS

2 slices cheese, ½–¾ inch thick
2–3 ounces deviled ham spread
1 teaspoon butter
Pinch of dry mustard

Cut slices of cheese into squares. With a melon ball cutter, grove center of each cheese square. Blend ham spread with butter and dry mustard. Place in pastry tube and squeeze a neat dab of the ham spread into each groove of the cheese square. Chill before serving.

12–18 PIECES

HORS D'OEUVRES 21

DIP FOR CUBED CHEESES

½ pound cheese, any firm variety
¼ cup mayonnaise
2 tablespoons prepared mustard
½ teaspoon dry mustard

Cut cheese into cubes; put on toothpicks. Blend other ingredients very well. Chill. Serve dressing in a small bowl, surrounded by cheese cubes.

MAKES ¼ CUP

DIP FOR LEFTOVER CUBED ROASTS

Use roast beef or steak, pork, ham, veal, tongue, lamb or meat loaf.

1 jar currant jelly (4 ounces)
2 teaspoons prepared mustard
Rind of 1 orange
Juice of ½ orange

Cut meat into cubes, as neatly as possible. Insert toothpicks. Blend other ingredients very well either with an electric beater or by hand. Chill. Serve meat cubes arranged around the bowl of dressing.

MAKES ½ CUP

DIPS FOR RABBIT FOOD

To accompany your dip use celery, carrots, zucchini and cauliflower, broken into flowerets.

Trim celery; scrape and cut into sticks. Scrape carrots and cut into sticks. Scrub zucchinis with a brush, then blanch by dropping into boiling salted water. After water has returned to the boiling point, drain immediately and chill. Trim off ends and cut into sticks lengthwise. Wrap all these well and chill. Trim cauliflowerets and drop them into cold salted water. Chill overnight or for a few hours. Dry all vegetables well with paper toweling. Arrange around a bowl filled with one of the following dressings:

½ cup sour cream
½ cup yoghurt
1 tablespoon finely chopped scallions or chives
Salt and pepper to taste

Mix all ingredients and chill.

MAKES 1 CUP

½ cup mayonnaise   *1 teaspoon grated onion*
½ cup sour cream   *Salt and pepper to taste*
3 tablespoons finely chopped
*   watercress (use stems only*
*   if desired)*

Mix all ingredients and chill.

MAKES 1 CUP

½ cup sour cream
4 ounces cream cheese at room temperature
4 tablespoons prepared horseradish, pressed very dry
4 tablespoons chili sauce

Work soft cream cheese into sour cream; add horseradish and chili sauce. Chill before serving.

MAKES 1 CUP

HORS D'OEUVRES   23

DIP FOR COOKED SHRIMP

This dip is also good with cold meats and other shellfish.

1–1½ pounds cooked shrimp,
peeled and deveined
½ cup chicken stock
1 tablespoon curry powder (or
more if a sharper taste is
desired)

4 teaspoons cornstarch
3–4 tablespoons water
½ cup mayonnaise
Salt and pepper to taste

Put shrimp on toothpicks and chill.

Combine chicken stock and curry powder; bring to the boiling point and simmer for 15 minutes. Blend cornstarch with water and add to simmering curry stock. Stir while cooking and thickening. When cornstarch is fully cooked, mixture will be clear. Remove from heat and cool to room temperature. Add mayonnaise and blend well. Chill before serving. Larger quantities may be prepared and stored for weeks.

MAKES ¾ CUP

SHRIMP SPREADS

8 ounces canned shrimp
1 tablespoon Durkee Famous Sauce

Mash shrimp with fork; blend in sauce. Place in bowl, cover with mayonnaise, and press a piece of waxed paper firmly over surface. Chill.

—or—

8 ounces canned shrimp
1 teaspoon lemon juice
1 teaspoon onion juice

½ teaspoon Worcestershire sauce
Mayonnaise

Mash shrimp with fork, add lemon and onion juices and the Worcestershire sauce. Add just enough mayonnaise to make a soft spread. Chill and store as above.

—or—

8 ounces canned shrimp
1 teaspoon lemon juice
Pinch of dry mustard
Commercial tartar sauce

Mash shrimp, add lemon juice, dry mustard and enough tartar sauce to make a smooth spread. Chill and store as above. Serve on toast, crackers or chips.

MAKES 1 CUP

CREAM CHEESE SPREADS

With Anchovies

6 ounces cream cheese (2 small packages)
1 can anchovies (2 ounces)

Soften cream cheese to room temperature. Drain and mash anchovies and gradually work in cream cheese. Place in bowl, spread a piece of waxed paper with a coating of butter, and press, buttered side down, firmly on the surface of the cream cheese mixture. Chill. Serve at room temperature on crackers. Will keep in refrigerator for 5 days.

MAKES ¾ CUP

With Olives and Nuts

6 ounces cream cheese (2 small packages)
1 tablespoon finely chopped nuts
1 tablespoon finely chopped olives

Combine cream cheese with olives and nuts. Store as above. Will keep in refrigerator for 3 days.

MAKES ¾ CUP

With Chives or Onions
1 tablespoon chives
6 ounces cream cheese
½ teaspoon onion juice or 2 tablespoons green herbs or scallions, chopped
Salt

Cut chives with scissors. Chop other herbs. Work into softened cream cheese, add onion juice and salt as desired. Store as above. Will keep in refrigerator for 24 hours.

MAKES ¾ CUP

COCKTAIL CHEESE PIE OR CAKE

CRUST:
1 stick butter (4 ounces), melted
1¼ cups sifted flour
1 raw egg

1 hard cooked egg yolk, rubbed through a sieve
½ teaspoon salt

Combine all ingredients and shape into a roll. Wrap in waxed paper and chill until just firm. Cut off slices and line a 9-inch spring mold cake pan with the dough, pressing down lightly when overlapping. Make a rim about ¾-inch high and scallop edge if desired. Prick the bottom very well to prevent bubbling. Bake 40 minutes in a moderate oven (325° F.) until lightly browned. Remove from pan when cool.

FILLING:

1 package plain gelatin
2 tablespoons water
½ cup milk
½ cup heavy cream
1 cup dry cottage cheese, known
    also as farmer or pot
    cheese

½ stick of butter (2 ounces) at
    room temperature
6 ounces Gorgonzola, or blue or
    Roquefort cheese, at room
    temperature.

Moisten gelatin with water, bring milk to the boiling point, add gelatin and dissolve. Cool. Add cream and chill until it begins to jell, then beat until fluffy. Rub cheese, butter and blue cheese through a sieve and add to the beaten milk–cream–gelatin mixture. Blend well. Pour into the cake shell and smooth surface. Chill, then garnish.

GARNISH:

Radish roses, sliced radishes, sliced blanched baby zucchini, walnut or pecan halves. These may be prepared the day before. Just before serving, a center of watercress sprigs may be added.

8–10 SERVINGS

SOUPS

SPARKLING CUCUMBER SOUP
(a variation of the Okroshka)

2 large cucumbers

3 hard cooked egg whites

1 bunch scallions

1 cup boiled ham, cut in julienne
    strips

1 cup cooked chicken or turkey
    meat cut in julienne strips

¾ cup light cream

3 hard cooked egg yolks rubbed
    through a sieve

1½ teaspoons dry mustard

½ teaspoon dry tarragon

1½ teaspoons salt

1½ teaspoons pepper

2½ teaspoons sugar

1 bottle of dry white wine, chilled

3 pint bottles club soda (total of
    1½ quarts), chilled

Peel cucumbers and split in half; with a teaspoon, remove seeds. Slice
very fine and place in a large bowl or soup tureen. Chop egg whites

and add to cucumbers. Trim scallions, wash, and snip with a pair of scissors into fine rings. Add to cucumbers together with the julienne cut ham and chicken or turkey. Combine cream, the sieved egg yolks, mustard, tarragon, salt, pepper and sugar. Just before serving, add wine and club soda. To prepare the night before, have all ingredients ready and combine just before serving.

MAKES 3 QUARTS

STRAWBERRY RASPBERRY SOUP

1 package frozen raspberries
  (*about 10 ounces*)
1 package frozen strawberries
  (*about 16 ounces*)

¼ cup sugar, if berries are sweet-
  ened, otherwise increase
¾ cup sour cream
¾ cup red wine, chilled
2 cups soda water (1 pint)

Defrost berries and either purée through a food mill or place in a blender to mash. Add sour cream and sugar. Mix well. Place in a soup tureen and just before serving add wine and soda water. (Fresh berries may be substituted, or this soup may be made from all strawberries or all raspberries.)

MAKES 1 QUART

RHUBARB SOUP

2 pounds rhubarb, without leaves
3 cups water
1½ cups sugar
1 stick cinnamon

GARNISH:

> 3 egg whites
> 4 tablespoons sugar

Cut young unpeeled rhubarb into 1 inch pieces. Peel older rhubarb and cut into 1 inch pieces. Wash and put into a wide 2-quart casserole with a very tight fitting cover. In a separate pot combine water, sugar and cinnamon and bring to the boiling point, uncovered. Reduce heat and simmer for 10 minutes, while beating egg whites until very stiff. Return the sugar water to the boiling point and pour over the rhubarb pieces. Again bring to the boiling point uncovered. Do not stir, keep at the boiling point for 30 seconds to ¾ minute. Turn off heat. Slide egg whites atop the rhubarb and sprinkle with the 4 tablespoons sugar. Cover tightly, and let stand for at least 30 minutes.

With a large spoon cut off dumplings from the egg whites and put them on a plate. Remove cinnamon stick and discard. Carefully transfer rhubarb to a soup tureen and garnish with the egg white dumplings. Serve at room temperature or chilled.

MAKES 2 QUARTS

GREEN PEA SOUP FRANÇAIS

> 3 tablespoons butter
> 3 cups shredded lettuce, washed
>   (use outer leaves if de-
>   sired)
> 1 onion, finely chopped (about
>   ½ cup)
> ¼ teaspoon nutmeg

> 5 cups chicken stock, fresh or
>   canned
> 2 packages frozen peas (10
>   ounces each)
> 2 teaspoons sugar
> ½ teaspoon pepper
> 2 teaspoons salt

GARNISH: Whipped heavy cream

Melt butter. Pat shredded lettuce dry with paper toweling and add to butter. Stir to coat lettuce, add onion and nutmeg and sauté over low heat until lettuce is wilted. Do not brown. In a 2-quart saucepan heat chicken stock; add peas, sautéed lettuce, sugar and salt and pepper. Simmer until peas are very soft, then rub the whole through a food mill or purée in blender. Chill and serve with a garnish of whipped heavy cream.

6 SERVINGS

AVOCADO CREAM SOUP

2 or 3 avocados, depending on size
4 cups chicken stock, fresh or
canned
½ cup sour cream ⎤ *or 1 cup milk or 1*
½ cup light cream ⎦ *cup Half & Half*

Salt and freshly ground pep-
per to taste
1 teaspoon grated onion
2 teaspoons fresh lemon juice

Peel avocados, remove seeds and mash, either by rubbing through a food mill or using a blender. Add chicken stock, sour and light creams, salt and pepper and grated onion. Blend well and chill. Add lemon juice just before serving.

6 SERVINGS

VICHYSSOISE

4–5 leeks, white part only
1 tablespoon chopped onion
2 ounces (½ stick) butter
½ teaspoon nutmeg
4 cups chicken stock
1 pound potatoes, washed, peeled
and sliced fine

½ cup heavy cream, chilled
½ cup Half & Half, chilled
Chilled milk to dilute further as
needed
Chopped chives

Trim and wash leeks very well; chop fine, mix with onions. Melt butter, add leeks and onions, sprinkle with nutmeg. Sauté over low heat until soft, but do not brown. In a quart casserole heat chicken stock, add sautéed leeks and onions, and potatoes. Simmer until potatoes are very soft. Rub the whole through a food mill or use a blender. Chill. Just before serving, mix with cream and Half & Half and dilute with milk as needed, depending on the mealiness of the potatoes used. Serve sprinkled with chopped chives.

MAKES 1½–2 QUARTS

SUMMER BORSCHT

¾ cup finely chopped onion
1½ cups chopped new cabbage
1 cup chopped carrots
2 ounces (½ stick) butter
2 cups chicken stock, fresh or
    canned

2 cups beef stock, fresh or canned
¼ cup malt or cider vinegar
2 cans (1 pound each) sliced
    beets or julienne cut red
    beets

GARNISH: 1½ pints sour cream

In a 4-quart saucepan combine onions, cabbage, carrots and butter. Over low heat, lightly brown the vegetables, about 10–15 minutes. Add chicken and beef stocks and vinegar and simmer for 10–15 minutes. Remove from heat. If sliced beets are used, drain the juice into the saucepan and chop the beets coarsely, then add to the mixture. If julienne beets are used, just add contents of cans to soup. For best results, chill overnight. Serve with plenty of sour cream.

MAKES 2½ QUARTS

TOMATO SOUP WITH HERBS

6 cups tomato juice, chilled
2 teaspoons oregano rubbed
    through a sieve
2 teaspoons salt

1 teaspoon basil, rubbed through
    a sieve
½ teaspoon pepper
1 cup sour cream

Combine all ingredients and blend very well. Chill for at least 4 hours, or overnight to allow flavors to develop. Garnish with either chopped chives or watercress.

MAKES 1½ QUARTS

TOMATO SOUP WITH CURRY

4 cups tomato juice
1 teaspoon curry powder (use
    more if desired)
3 tablespoons tomato paste
1 teaspoon salt

½ teaspoon basil
¼ teaspoon pepper
3 tablespoons lemon juice
1 cup sour cream
3 tablespoons chopped parsley

Heat tomato juice, add curry powder and simmer for 10 minutes. Add tomato paste, salt, basil and pepper and stir to dissolve paste. Chill. Just before serving add lemon juice and sour cream. Stir to blend well. Garnish with chopped parsley.

MAKES 1¼ QUARTS

DILLED TOMATO SOUP

1 can (1 pound) peeled tomatoes	*1 teaspoon salt*
½ cup chopped onions	*½ teaspoon pepper*
1 sliver garlic	*3 sprigs fresh dill*
½ cup instant potatoes	*½ cup Half & Half*
1 cup chicken stock, fresh or	
canned	

In a 3-quart saucepan combine tomatoes, onions, garlic, potatoes, chicken stock and salt and pepper. Simmer over low heat for 20 minutes. Rub through a food mill or use blender. Chill overnight. Just before serving add finely snipped dill and cream; blend well.

MAKES 1 QUART

CURRIED CREAM OF CELERY SOUP

2 cups milk	*¼ cup melted butter*
2 cans cream of celery soup	*Salt and pepper to taste*
3 teaspoons curry powder	*Grated salted peanuts*

Combine milk and soup and bring to the boiling point. Combine curry and melted butter and add. Simmer for 10 minutes. Taste for seasonings. Chill. Serve with a garnish of grated salted peanuts.

MAKES 1 QUART

JEAN THACKREY'S SPECIAL SPINACH SOUP

*1 package frozen spinach (10
    ounces)
Good pinch of nutmeg
1 small onion, coarsely chopped
3 tablespoons butter*

*1 can double-strength chicken
    broth
2 cups milk
Salt to taste*

Cook spinach according to instructions on package, but add nutmeg. Sauté onion in butter until softened, but do not brown. Combine cooked spinach, onion and soup in the blender and purée until very smooth. Add milk, season to taste and chill.

MAKES 1½ QUARTS

JELLIED SOUPS

BASIC STOCK

*1½ pounds oxtails
2 pounds chicken backs
2 cups soup greens or trimmings
    from celery, lettuce, a few
    carrots, parsley or parsley
    stems*

*2 onions stuck with a clove
14 cups water (3½ quarts)
1 bay leaf
6 peppercorns
2 tablespoons salt*

Combine all ingredients in a 5–6 gallon casserole and simmer for 4 hours. Strain through a sieve; discard bones, vegetables and spices. Set stock to cool, then chill. Remove all fat.

MAKES 4 QUARTS

JELLIED CONSOMMÉ

8 cups of Basic Stock
2 packages plain gelatin
½ cup cold water
3 egg whites, beaten until frothy

Crushed eggshells from 3 eggs
1 tablespoon caramel coloring or
gravy coloring

Bring the jellied stock to the boiling point. Soften gelatin in water for 5 minutes, then add to stock together with frothy egg whites, shells and coloring. Stirring with a wire whisk, cook over high heat until stock begins to foam. Remove from heat and let stand for 5–8 minutes. Line a large colander with a damp cloth and strain liquid into a large pot. Do not disturb in any way. When all is run through, taste for seasonings and chill. Break jellied consommé up with a spoon and serve in soup cups. Garnish with a slice of lemon. Or pour liquid into a flat cake pan and chill and dice.

MAKES 2 QUARTS

MADRILÈNE

Substitute 4 cups of fresh or canned tomatoes for 4 cups of unclarified stock. Simmer for 15 minutes before bringing the stock to the boiling point and adding the gelatin and egg whites. Then proceed as above.

4 SERVINGS

RED PEPPER JELLIED CONSOMMÉ

Prepare Basic Stock, page 35. After clarifying, add the purée of a 4-ounce can of pimientos to the clarified soup. (To purée, rub through a sieve or use blender.) Then add ½ cup sherry and ⅛ teaspoon cayenne pepper.

4 SERVINGS

RED BEET JELLIED CONSOMMÉ

To jellied consommé made from 8 cups of stock add 1 cup julienne cut red beets (canned). Garnish with sour cream.

4 SERVINGS

JELLIED CREAM OF CHICKEN SOUP

Use either jelled chicken stock, left over from cooking a chicken for salad or use basic soup stock. See page 35.

6 cups of jelled stock, free of fat
4 tablespoons heavy cream or sour cream
3 tablespoons sherry wine
A few watercress leaves for garnish.

Heat stock until liquified, add cream and beat until smooth. Add sherry. Chill until set again. Beat again. Divide between 6 cups and drop a few watercress leaves on top.

6 SERVINGS

WINE SOUP

3 cups water	1 cup sugar
1 bottle white wine, dry	1 stick cinnamon
½ teaspoon salt	4 egg yolks

Combine the 3 cups water with half the wine; add salt, sugar and cinnamon and simmer for 15 minutes. Remove and discard cinnamon. Beat remaining wine with egg yolks and add to the liquid. Reheat to just below the boiling point. Chill well. Serve with salt pretzels.

MAKES 1½ QUARTS

CREAMED CARROT SOUP

1½ cups chopped carrots	1 teaspoon salt
½ cup chopped onions	½ teaspoon pepper
½ cup chopped celery	2 tablespoons quick-cooking rice
3 cups chicken stock, fresh or canned	1 cup Half & Half

Combine carrots, onions, celery, stock, salt and pepper in a 2-quart saucepan and simmer until vegetables are soft. Add rice and simmer for 5 more minutes. Rub through a food mill or use blender. Chill overnight. Just before serving add Half & Half and mix well.

MAKES 1½ QUARTS

EMILY HAMMOND'S PARSLEY SOUP

2 cups parsley tops, tightly packed
1 package fresh spinach (10
    ounces) or 1 package
    frozen spinach (10
    ounces)
Water
2 cups milk

1 medium red Bermuda onion,
    sliced
1 teaspoon salt
½ teaspoon pepper
¼ teaspoon rosemary
Sour cream
Paprika

Wash parsley and pat dry. Wash fresh spinach, remove all hard stems and put in a large pot. Bring about 2 cups water to the boiling point, pour over spinach, return to the boiling point and simmer for 1 minute. Drain and press lightly. If using frozen spinach, defrost, but do not blanch. Pour ½ cup milk into blender and gradually add parsley tops, spinach and sliced onion. If blender gets too full pour out puréed part and start all over again with another ½ cup milk. Finally add salt, pepper and rosemary. Pour into a bowl and add remaining milk. Chill. Serve with a dab of sour cream garnished with a dash of paprika.

MAKES 1 QUART

Note: If a thinner soup is desired, add more milk.

BUTTERMILK SOUP

2 slices very dark pumpernickel
    bread
½ cup sugar

1 quart buttermilk
½ cup light cream
6 Zwieback or rusk

Toast pumpernickel until quite dry, then crush in blender. Add sugar and set aside. Mix buttermilk and light cream. Crush Zwieback or

rusk and add to milk. Chill. Serve in soup bowls and sprinkle with
the pumpernickel–sugar mixture.

6 SERVINGS

STRAWBERRY SOUP

*2 baskets of fresh strawberries or use 3 packages (10 ounces each)
    frozen*
4 tablespoons sugar—omit if using sweetened frozen berries
1 pint milk ⎱
1 pint light cream ⎰ *or use all milk*

Wash and hull berries. Cut them in half, but put aside 12 whole
berries for garnish. Sprinkle with sugar. Defrost frozen berries. Combine milk and cream. Put some of the berries in the blender; add some
of the milk and purée. Repeat until all berries are used up. Pour in
a saucepan and over very low heat bring close to the boiling point,
but do not boil. (Watch for the little bubbles on the side.) Remove
from heat and chill. Garnish with the whole berries.

6 SERVINGS

THRIFTY SOUP

Don't throw out the trimmings of a stalk of celery, leaves and all; the
trimmings of lettuce, any kind; stems of watercress or parsley; slices
of tomatoes or pulp; trimmings from scallions; even the peel of
washed carrots. Just save them up and then make Thrifty Soup.

4 cups celery leaves and trim-   *2 cups salad-green trimmings*
    mings from celery   *1 onion stuck with 2 cloves*
  1 cup parsley and watercress   *1 carrot*
    stems

1 white turnip or parsnip	1 teaspoon peppercorns
Tomato trimmings	2 tablespoons cream of wheat
Scallion trimmings	½ white turnip, coarsely grated
7 cups water	½ carrot, coarsely grated
1 tablespoon salt	Sour cream

In a large pot combine celery trimmings, parsley, salad greens, onion and carrot. Add whatever else is available. Then add water, salt and peppercorns. Bring to the boiling point and simmer for 30–40 minutes. Strain; press down lightly to extract the liquid from the vegetables. Discard vegetables. Bring liquid to the boiling point, add cream of wheat and simmer to thicken, about 10 minutes. Add grated carrots and turnips, return to boiling point, then cool and chill. Add a dab of sour cream to each serving.

MAKES 8 CUPS OR 6 SOUP PLATES

CHERRY SOUP

2 pounds cherries or use frozen cherries, about 18 ounces, depending on packaging	¼ cup water
	¼ cup red wine
	Juice and peel of 1 lemon
¾ cup sugar, or less if sugared frozen fruit is used	2 teaspoons cornstarch
	Sour cream or whipped cream

Pit cherries in a bowl, sprinkle with sugar and let stand for several hours until they have formed some juice. Drain off juice and reserve. Combine cherries, water and wine in a saucepan, squeeze out lemon juice, add to cherries. Bring to the boiling point and simmer for 3–4 minutes. Blend drained-off cherry juice with the cornstarch and add to saucepan. Simmer until thickened. Remove lemon rinds; chill cherries. Serve garnished with sour cream or whipped cream.

6 SERVINGS

FISH AND SHELLFISH

FISH PUDDING WITH MORNING GLORY SAUCE

PUDDING:

1 pound fish, frozen or fresh	*½ teaspoon pepper*
Juice of 1 lime	*White wine*
1 cup white wine	*2 envelopes plain gelatin*
1 cup water	*¾ cup mayonnaise*
1 bay leaf	*Salt and pepper to taste*
1 tablespoon instant onions	*¾ cup finely chopped celery*
1 teaspoon salt	*2 tablespoons drained capers*

SAUCE:

4 egg yolks	*Juice of 2 lemons*
1 stick butter (¼ pound)	*2 tablespoons tomato paste*
¾ teaspoon salt	*3 tablespoons mayonnaise*

Defrost frozen fish, rinse fresh fish, and sprinkle with lime juice. Combine white wine, water, bay leaf, instant onions, salt and pepper and simmer for 15 minutes. Add the fish and poach for 5–10 minutes depending on thickness of fish used. Remove bay leaf and chill.

Drain liquid from fish and measure. Add enough white wine to make 2½ cups. Put ½ cup in a small saucepan, sprinkle the 2 envelopes of plain gelatin over it. Heat gently, stirring constantly to dissolve gelatin. Add to the remaining 2 cups liquid, stir, add mayonnaise, taste for seasoning and pour into two refrigerator ice cube trays. Chill until it begins to set. Put in a bowl and beat with an electric beater. Place in the refrigerator (but not in the freezing compartment) for just a few minutes, then beat again. Repeat until very fluffy. Crumble fish and then add with celery and capers. Put into a fancy quart mold or divide between 4 1-cup molds or 8 ½-cup molds. Chill to set, preferably overnight.

Unmold by dipping in warm water and reversing on a service platter.

For the sauce: Put egg yolks in the blender; beat. Melt butter but do not let brown. Add to blender and beat; add salt, lemon juice, tomato paste, and blend again. Add mayonnaise. Blend. Pour into a container and chill until ready to serve.

MAKES 1 QUART

FISH PILLOWS IN ASPIC

8 small slices filet of sole or filet of
*   flounder*
Juice 1 lemon
1 can mushrooms, pieces and stems
*   (4 ounces)*

1 can minced clams (8 ounces)
¼ teaspoon tarragon leaves, dry
White wine

ASPIC:

> *White wine*
> *1 envelope plain gelatin*
> *2 teaspoons cornstarch*

Heat oven to 375° F. Rinse filets, arrange on a cookie sheet and sprinkle with lemon juice. Drain mushrooms and clams, reserve liquids. Put 3 tablespoons of this liquid into a blender; add mushrooms and clams and purée. This makes about 1 cup.

Divide this mixture between the 8 filets, placing each portion in the middle of the filet. Fold over from both sides, making a pillow. Set these folded side down into a baking dish, setting them close together. To the strained liquids add tarragon and pour over pillows. Add enough white wine to cover them halfway up. Cover with aluminum foil and bake for 25 minutes. Remove from oven, uncover, cool and then chill, covered with plastic wrap. After 3–4 hours or the next day place fish pillows on a flat surface. Strain and measure baking liquid. Add enough white wine to make 1 cup. Put in a small saucepan, sprinkle gelatin over it and add cornstarch. Bring to the boiling point over low heat, stirring constantly. Let cool slightly, then coat the pillows. Repeat once more. If coating gets too thick reheat gently. If desired, decorate with a sprig of dill or a small piece of pimiento. Chill before serving.

8 SERVINGS

FILET OF FLOUNDER OR SOLE
WITH SHRIMP AND BRANDIED MAYONNAISE

8 filets of flounder or sole, fresh	1 teaspoon instant onions
Juice of 1 lemon	1 teaspoon salt
8 large shrimp	Toothpicks
3 cups water	2 envelopes plain gelatin
1 bay leaf	1½ cups white wine

MAYONNAISE:

2 eggs	½ teaspoon pepper
1 cup oil	2 teaspoons dry mustard
1 teaspoon salt	Juice of 1 lemon
1 teaspoon sugar	2 tablespoons brandy

Rinse filets of flounder or sole, sprinkle with lemon juice. Do not defrost frozen shrimp. Bring water, combined with bay leaf, onion and salt to the boiling point, reduce to simmer and cook for 20 minutes. Raise heat to the boiling point and drop in shrimp. Keep on high heat and as soon as liquid returns to boiling point, drain shrimp and reserve the liquid.

Cool shrimp. Wrap a filet of fish around each shrimp; secure with toothpicks. Measure 1½ cups of the shrimp cooking liquid, sprinkle with gelatin and heat gently, stirring constantly until gelatin is dissolved. Add the 1½ cups white wine.

Heat oven to 375° F. Arrange fish rolls in a fireproof dish or mold, one that holds about 4–5 cups (a large bread pan or a round baking casserole is fine). Pour the liquid over the fish rolls and set in the preheated oven. Bake for 20 minutes. Remove from oven, cool, and before setting in the refrigerator to chill, turn all the toothpicks up. This will make it easy to remove them from the jellied rolls. Either unmold the whole, then cut the fish rolls apart, or cut them apart while still in the mold. Decorate with sprigs of dill or a strip of pimiento.

If individual molds are desired, chill the whole until well cooled (the fish rolls are very fragile while warm), then set the rolls into individual molds and divide the baking liquid between them.

To make the mayonnaise: put eggs in blender and beat, add ¼ cup of oil and beat gradually, add salt, sugar, pepper, dry mustard remaining oil, and beat. Add lemon juice and brandy, beating after each addition. Pour into service dish and chill before serving.

8 SERVINGS

OCEAN PERCH OR ROSEFISH FILETS WITH GRAPEFRUIT

4 fish filets, about 1 pound　　　*2 bay leaves*
Juice of 1 lime　　　　　　　　*1 teaspoon salt*
1 can unsweetened grapefruit sec-　*Grapefruit juice*
*　　tions (16 ounces)*

COATING:

White wine
1 envelope plain gelatin
2 teaspoons cornstarch
Pecan halves, optional

Heat oven to 375° F. Remove skin from filets. Arrange fish on a flat surface and sprinkle with lime juice. Drain grapefruit, reserve liquid. Arrange 2 filets in a small baking dish, and divide grapefruit sections between the two filets, arranging all over the top. Place remaining filets on top of them, sandwich fashion. Add bay leaves. Add salt to drained-off grapefruit juice and pour over filets to cover.

46　　FISH AND SHELLFISH

Cover tightly with baking-dish lid or aluminum foil. Bake 30 minutes. Remove cover and cool, then cover with plastic wrap and chill.

Either leave filets whole or divide each into two or three portions. Arrange these portions on a flat surface. Strain cooking liquid, measure off 1 cup and if there is not enough, add white wine. Place this 1 cup liquid into a small saucepan, sprinkle with gelatin and add cornstarch. Bring to the boiling point over low heat, stirring constantly. Remove from heat and let cool slightly. Then coat whole filets or portions all over. Repeat once. If coating liquid gets too thick, reheat gently. If desired, decorate before coating with whole pecan halves. Chill before serving.

8 SERVINGS

TUNA FISH SALAD

1 can tuna fish (6½–7 ounces)	*1 tablespoon grated onion*
1 apple	*Juice ½ lemon*
2 tablespoons mayonnaise	*Salt and pepper to taste*

Drain tuna fish and flake. Peel apple, cut in quarters and remove core. Use the coarsest side of a household grater to shred apple quarters. Combine tuna with apple shreds, mayonnaise, grated onion and lemon juice. Mix and taste for seasonings. Chill. Serve on tomato or avocado slices.

6 SERVINGS

DOUBLE MOLD TUNA FISH SALAD

1 can tuna fish (6½–7 ounces)
1 can green asparagus (8¼
ounces)
1 bottle clam juice (8 ounces)

2 envelopes plain gelatin
3 cups Clamato juice
2 envelopes gelatin

Select 2 molds, one about 4–5 cups that will fit loosely over a 3-cup mold.

Drain tuna, rinse and crumble. Drain asparagus, cut into small pieces and reserve liquid. Combine tuna fish and asparagus. Measure asparagus liquid, add enough clam juice and water to make 2 cups. Put ½ cup of combined liquid into a small saucepan, sprinkle gelatin on top, heat gently, and stir until gelatin is dissolved. Add to other liquids, then add to tuna fish and asparagus. Fill the smaller mold. Chill. When mold is set, loosen edges, dip in warm water and unmold on a plate. Then, put the larger mold over it and reverse. Center the aspic mold. Pour ½ cup of the 3 cups Clamato juice into a small saucepan, sprinkle gelatin over it, heat gently and stir constantly to dissolve gelatin. Pour this and the rest of the juice into a large saucepan and reheat to "baby bottle heat" (a drop will feel comfortable on the wrist). Add this bottle-warm juice to the larger mold with the aspic; spoon in gently at first, then pour over and cover. Set to chill overnight. To unmold: loosen the edges, then place mold in warm water and count to ten. Reverse onto large platter. Garnish with watercress and serve with the following dressing:

1 cup creamed cottage cheese (8
ounces)
3–4 tablespoons milk
Juice of 1 lemon

½ cup mayonnaise
1 teaspoon salt
1 teaspoon dry mustard
4 tablespoons frozen chives

Combine all ingredients in a blender in the order given, blending after each addition. Add chives last and blend just a few seconds.

8 SERVINGS

CURRIED TUNA FISH ASPIC

1 bottle clam juice (8 ounces)　　*1 can tuna fish (6 ounces)*
1 teaspoon curry powder　　　　*2 tablespoons chopped nuts, any*
½ cup water　　　　　　　　　　　*variety*
1 package plain gelatin　　　　　*1 banana*

Combine clam juice and curry powder in a small saucepan and bring to the boiling point. Simmer for 5 minutes to develop curry flavor. Sprinkle gelatin over ½ cup water to soften; add to clam juice and stir to dissolve. Rinse tuna fish with hot water to remove oil. Add to the clam juice together with the chopped nuts.

Set aside the mixture to cool, then chill until it begins to jell. Peel banana, cut in half through middle, then cut each half lengthwise. Cut each of the halves into strips, then dice. Add to tuna fish mixture and divide between 4 custard cups or other fancy small molds. Chill until set. Remove from molds and decorate with a small dab of mayonnaise.

4 SERVINGS

TUNA FISH PIE

2 cans tuna fish (6½–7 ounces)　　*½ cup white wine*
1 can unsweetened grapefruit sec-　*Water*
tions (16 ounces)　　　　　　　　*2 envelopes plain gelatin*
1 bag chopped pecans or walnuts
(3½ ounces)

GARNISH:

1 cup mayonnaise
⅔ cup grapefruit juice
1 envelope plain gelatin

Drain tuna fish and crumble into an 8- or 9-inch pie pan. Drain grapefruit sections, reserve juice, cut grapefruit sections in half and add to tuna fish. Sprinkle chopped pecans over it and mix well, distributing the mixture evenly over the pie pan.

Measure grapefruit juice. Add ½ cup white wine and enough water to make 2 cups. Place half a cup of this liquid into a small saucepan, sprinkle with the gelatin and over low heat, stirring constantly, heat until gelatin is dissolved. Add to the other liquid mixture and spoon over tuna fish mixture. Chill to set overnight.

To decorate: put mayonnaise in a bowl and chill. Put grapefruit juice in a small saucepan, sprinkle gelatin over it and heat gently, stirring constantly, until gelatin is dissolved. Let this mixture cool to raw egg white consistency. (To hasten, set in a bowl of ice and stir occasionally.) Combine with chilled mayonnaise, place in pastry bag and make a lattice pattern over the jellied tuna fish pie. Chill before serving.

Cut into 6 or 8 portions and serve like a pie.

CLAMATO CODFISH FILETS

2 pounds codfish filets (not steaks)	*1 can baby sliced tomatoes (14½ ounces)*
1 lemon, halved	*2 envelopes plain gelatin*
1 can Clamato juice (16 ounces)	

Preheat oven to 375°–400° F. Rub filets with lemon, then cut the filets into 6 equal portions. Arrange them in a baking dish with a rim. Pour the Clamato juice over it, then strain the liquid from the baby tomatoes over the whole, straining out seeds. Cover with aluminum foil. Bake for 20–25 minutes. Remove from oven, cool and chill in the baking dish. After about 2 hours remove filets to a rimmed cookie sheet. Measure liquid, there should be about 2 cups. Place ½ cup of this liquid in a saucepan, sprinkle gelatin over it, heat gently and stir constantly until gelatin is dissolved. Add to remaining liquid. Spoon some of the liquid over filets. Arrange tomatoes on top as a garnish. Spoon some more gelatin liquid over the whole. Chill, then repeat once more, making sure all is covered with gelatin. Chill before serving. Any leftover liquid can be chilled and chopped after chilling and used as a garnish.

6 SERVINGS

CRABMEAT SALAD

2 cans crabmeat (6½–7 ounces)	½ small green pepper
or fresh, about 1 pound	4 anchovy filets
Juice of 1 lemon	2 ounces pimientos (small jar)
1 package of frozen lima beans	1 cup mayonnaise
(10 ounces)	Salt and pepper to taste

Drain crabmeat, pick over and sprinkle with lemon juice. Chill. Cook lima beans according to instructions on package, drain and chill. Remove seeds and white membrane from green pepper and chop coarsely in blender. Add anchovies, pimientos and mayonnaise and blend for one second, just enough to mix. Combine mayonnaise with crabmeat and lima beans.

Serve on sliced tomatoes, or sliced cucumbers and sliced tomatoes, or spoon into avocado shells or scooped-out tomatoes.

8 SERVINGS

SALMON AND CUCUMBER MOLD

1 *can salmon (7½–7¾ ounces)*
1 *cucumber*
1 *tablespoon salt*
½ *cup fresh dill leaves, loosely packed*
½ *teaspoon pepper*
4 *ounces sour cream*
Water
2 *envelopes plain gelatin*

Drain salmon, crumble and place in a bowl; set aside to chill. Peel cucumber, remove seeds and put them in a sieve set over a bowl. Cut up cucumber and sprinkle with salt. Let stand 1 hour, then drain and place in blender. Add dill and pepper and purée. Add sour cream and pour over salmon. Press the seeds and pulp from cucumber through sieve to extract all liquid. Measure liquid and add enough water to make 1 cup. Put this liquid in a small saucepan, sprinkle the gelatin on top and heat gently, stirring constantly, until gelatin is dissolved. Add to the salmon mixture and mix. This makes about 3 cups. Pour into one fancy mold such as a fish mold or divide between four to six small molds. Chill overnight to set.

To unmold, loosen around edges. Dip mold in a pan with warm water, count to ten, and reverse onto a service platter.

SALMON SALAD IN CUCUMBERS

½–¾ *pound fresh salmon, preferably a tail end piece*
Juice of 1 lemon
2 *cucumbers, medium size*
2 *cups water*
1 *tablespoon tarragon vinegar*
1 *bay leaf*
½ *teaspoon dry dill weed*
2 *teaspoons salt*
1 *envelope plain gelatin*
1 *cup mayonnaise*

Rinse salmon and sprinkle with lemon juice. Peel cucumbers, cut in half and remove seeds. Put seeds and pulp into a saucepan large enough to hold the fish. Add water, vinegar, bay leaf, dill and salt. Bring to the boiling point and simmer for 30 minutes. Reserving the ends, cut from the 4 cucumber halves 4 troughs, each about 4 inches long. Drop these into the simmering broth, raise heat and bring to the boiling point. Remove cucumber troughs; cool and chill. Drop fish into the broth and simmer, do not boil, for 20–30 minutes, depending on thickness of the fish cuts. Fish should be covered with liquid; if not, add more water. Remove fish and drain liquid through a very fine sieve. Measure off ⅔ cup and discard remainder. Put the ⅔ cup liquid into a small saucepan and sprinkle with gelatin. Heat gently, stirring constantly, until gelatin is dissolved. Cool, then chill. Watch this carefully and stir occasionally while cooling to the consistency of raw egg white. If in a hurry, set over ice and stir. As soon as liquid has the right consistency, mix with mayonnaise. Remove bones and skin from the fish and break into large pieces. Chop the cucumber ends coarsely and add to fish. Mix fish and chopped cucumber with about ¾ of the gelatin mayonnaise. Fill into troughs, piling high. Put the remainder of the gelatin mayonnaise into a pastry bag; chill for 20 minutes. Then pipe a decorative design over the filled cucumbers. For further decoration use either fresh dill sprigs or dots of pimiento or sliced olives. Chill before serving.

4 SERVINGS

SHRIMP IN GRAPEFRUIT SHELLS

3 grapefruits
4 cups water
1 bay leaf
1 tablespoon instant onion
Stems from a small bunch of dill

2 teaspoons salt
1½ pounds frozen shrimp
Grapefruit juice
1 envelope plain gelatin

1 egg	*½ teaspoon pepper*
½ cup oil	*Leaves from a bunch of dill (about*
½ cup heavy cream	*½ cup)*
1 teaspoon salt	

Cut grapefruit in half, remove sections and drain off juice. Chill sections and juice. Remove center part from grapefruit shell and chill shells. Bring water, bay leaf, onions, dill stems and salt to the boiling point. Reduce heat and simmer for 20 minutes. Bring to the boiling point, place frozen shrimp into another saucepan and strain boiling liquid over them. Bring back to the boiling point over high heat. As soon as liquid is boiling and foaming, drain off shrimp. Cool and chill. Measure 1 cup of grapefruit juice. Put ½ cup of this juice into a small saucepan, sprinkle with gelatin, and over low heat, stirring constantly, dissolve gelatin. Combine with other ½ cup juice and chill, until it has the consistency of raw egg white. (If in a hurry, set in a bowl of ice.) Now make your dressing. In the blender beat egg, gradually add oil and when thickened, add heavy cream, salt, pepper, and the partially jelled grapefruit juice. Blend, then add dill leaves and quickly chop them. The sauce will now be light green. Pour into a bowl and chill until it has the consistency of mayonnaise. Combine chilled shrimp and chilled grapefruit sections. Add enough of the dressing to bind. Divide between the chilled grapefruit shells and serve remaining dressing on the side.

6 SERVINGS

SALMON IN RED WINE

1 can salmon (7½–7¾ ounces)	*Water*
1 cup red wine	*2 envelopes of plain gelatin*
Juice of 1 lime	*4 ounces sour cream*
1 can mushroom stems and pieces	*1 teaspoon salt*
(4 ounces)	*½ teaspoon pepper*

Drain salmon, put in blender with red wine and lime juice and purée. Put in a bowl. Drain mushrooms, add the stems and pieces to the salmon and measure drained-off liquid. Add enough water to make 1 cup. Put this liquid into a small saucepan, sprinkle gelatin over it and over low heat, stirring constantly, dissolve gelatin. Add this to salmon, blend in, then add sour cream, salt and pepper. Mix. Put into one fancy mold such as a fish mold or divide between four to six individual molds. Chill overnight.

To unmold, loosen edges, then set in a pan with warm water, count to ten, and reverse onto a service platter.

MAKES ABOUT 3½ CUPS

POACHED SALMON IN ASPIC

1 whole salmon (approximately 6 pounds)	*10 cups water*
Lemons	*1 bay leaf*
Stems of fresh dill, a few sprigs parsley, a few celery tops, 1 carrot, 1 onion stuck with a clove	*4 tablespoons salt*
	3 cups white wine
	Roasting pan and cheesecloth

COATING:

5 cups cooking liquid
5 envelopes plain gelatin
1 egg white and shell

Wash salmon, rub inside with lemon and keep refrigerated. Combine water, dill, parsley, celery, carrot, onion, bay leaf and salt in a large pot and simmer for 1–2 hours. This can be done the day before. Strain the liquid. Line a roasting pan with double thickness of cheesecloth. Allow a generous overlap at both ends. Place salmon on top. Pour white wine over it, then fill up with enough of the vegetable broth to cover fish completely. Place pan over two burners, bring to the boiling point, then turn down immediately to a simmer. Cover. Watch carefully that fish liquid does not boil but stays at a simmer. Simmer for 45 minutes at the most. A small fish or a thinner fish will take less time. To test whether it is done, scrape off a small piece of the skin and lift the flesh. Use potholders and grasp the overlap of the cheese-cloth. Gently lift the fish from the water to a service platter. Wipe off any remaining liquid with paper towels. While still on the cheesecloth remove skin from one side, scraping gently if necessary. Remove the peeled-off skin with paper towels. Turn the platter so that the belly side is nearest you. Pull fish toward you, then lift the belly side and turn fish over, using the heavier backside as a pivot. Scrape off skin from other side, wipe platter clean, discard cheesecloth (or it can be washed and used again). Chill fish.

Cool 5 cups of cooking liquid, sprinkle with gelatin, beat egg white and add along with shell. Slowly bring to the boiling point, stirring often. When it boils remove from heat and let settle. Strain through a double thickness of kitchen toweling. Let cool and chill but do not allow to jell. When it begins to thicken coat the chilled fish all over with the liquid. Repeat until a good, shiny coat has been built up. Chill.

For decoration: the classic decoration is sliced cucumber. Peel and slice a cucumber, dip in the coating and arrange over and around the fish while coating. If the cucumbers slide off, secure with toothpicks and repeat coating. Remove toothpicks after coating is set. Any coating that has dripped to the platter can be removed easily after it is set by lifting off with a knife. Serve with dill sauce or horseradish sauce.

Other fish such as bass or red snapper may be prepared in the same manner. If a cucumber garnish is not desired, use sprigs of dill.

Dill Sauce for Poached Salmon (or Other Fish)

3 tablespoons Durkee Famous
    Sauce
1 cup mayonnaise
1 cup fresh dill leaves and thin
    stems, loosely packed (use

coarse stems in the broth
    for the salmon)
½ cup sour cream
½ cup plain yoghurt
1 teaspoon salt

In the blender, combine Durkee Famous Sauce and ½ cup mayonnaise with the dill leaves. Blend for a few seconds at low speed until the dill is finely chopped. Drain from blender, add all other ingredients and mix gently. Pour into service bowl, cover and set aside to chill.

MAKES ABOUT 2 CUPS

Horseradish Sauce for Poached Salmon (or Other Fish)

½ pint (1 cup) heavy cream
4 ounces hot bottled horseradish
½ teaspoon salt or more to taste

Whip cream. Drain horseradish and press dry. Add to whipped cream and season with salt to taste. Place in service bowl, cover and chill.

MAKES ABOUT 2 CUPS

BEER SHRIMP SALAD IN AVOCADO SHELLS

2 cans beer
2 tablespoons salt
2 bay leaves

1 tablespoon dehydrated onion
1½ pounds frozen shrimp
3 avocados

FISH AND SHELLFISH   57

DRESSING:

1 hard cooked egg yolk	*1 raw egg yolk*
½ cup heavy cream	*2 teaspoons dry mustard*
1 teaspoon salt	*2 teaspoons sugar*
½ teaspoon pepper	*3 tablespoons tarragon vinegar*

Combine beer, salt, bay leaves, and onions and simmer for 20 minutes. Drop frozen shrimp into the broth and over high heat return to the boiling point. Remove immediately and drain the shrimp. Cool and chill. Prepare the dressing: Press hard cooked egg yolk through a sieve and reserve. Beat heavy cream until quite stiff, then add hard cooked egg yolk, salt, pepper, raw egg yolk, mustard, sugar and vinegar. Beat until well blended, then place in a bowl and chill. Add enough of this dressing to coat the shrimp. Cut avocados in half, remove seeds. Fill with the shrimp salad and pipe remaining dressing around the rim of the avocados.

6 SERVINGS

SHRIMP AND EGGS IN ASPIC

4 hard cooked eggs	*Juice of 2 lemons*
1 can shrimp, medium or small	*Salt and pepper to taste*
(4½ ounces)	*1 tablespoon chopped pimientos*
½ teaspoon whole pickling spice	*1 tablespoon chopped parsley*
1 cup water	*2 scallions, white and green parts,*
1 envelope plain gelatin	*chopped*
¾ cup water	

Quarter the hard cooked eggs. Drain and rinse shrimp. Add pickling spice to 1 cup water, bring to the boiling point, then simmer for 10 minutes. Sprinkle gelatin over the ¾ cup water, mix, then add lemon juice. Strain the boiling spiced water over the gelatin water and stir to dissolve. Taste for seasonings.

Use either 4 1-cup molds or 8 ½-cup molds. Divide quartered eggs between them, either 4 or 2 for each mold. Mix together pimientos, parsley, and scallions and sprinkle some into each mold, then add the rest to the shrimp. Mix and divide shrimp between molds; then pour the gelatin liquid over the molds. Chill overnight.

FISH SALAD WITH AVOCADO SAUCE

2 pounds halibut	1 bay leaf
3 cups water	Stems from a small bunch of dill
1 tablespoon instant onion	1 tablespoon vinegar

SAUCE:

1 very ripe avocado	1 teaspoon salt
3 tablespoons grated onion	½ teaspoon pepper
2 tablespoons lemon juice	2 tablespoons mayonnaise

Rinse fish. Combine water, onion, bay leaf, dill stems and vinegar and bring to the boiling point. Simmer for 15 minutes, then add fish. Poach for 15–20 minutes depending on thickness of fish cut.

Remove fish from cooking broth, but save broth. Cool fish slightly, remove skin and bones and keep fish in as large pieces as possible. Place pieces in a bowl and strain enough cooking liquid over them to cover well. Chill.

To make the sauce: Remove meat from avocado; place in the blender. Add grated onion, lemon juice, salt, pepper and mayonnaise. Blend until smooth. Chill.

Drain fish from liquid. Break into bite-sized pieces. Add avocado sauce and mix gently. Arrange on lettuce leaves. If desired, garnish with fresh dill leaves or sliced eggs.

6 SERVINGS

SCALLOPS AND CELERY SALAD

2 *pounds scallops*   ¼ *teaspoon pepper*
5 *tablespoons white wine*   *Mayonnaise*
2 *cups finely diced celery*   *Chopped fresh dill or parsley*
1 *teaspoon salt*

Rinse scallops. Place in a saucepan, add wine and over low heat gently poach scallops for about 5 minutes; they will give out liquid. Let cool, then chill in liquid. Drain very well. Cut small scallops in half, quarter larger ones. Mix with celery, sprinkle lightly with salt and pepper and add just enough mayonnaise to bind.

If available, serve in individual scallop shells, otherwise on lettuce leaves. Garnish with chopped dill or parsley.

MAKES 1 QUART

LOBSTER SALAD ON GRAPEFRUIT SOCLE

3 *packages frozen lobster tails, 7 ounces each*

BROTH:

3–4 *cups water*   2 *teaspoons salt*
1 *bay leaf*   *Stems of a small bunch of dill*
2 *teaspoons instant onion*

SOCLE:

2 *small grapefruits*

DRESSING:

¾ *cup mayonnaise*
Leaves from a small bunch of dill.

Remove tails from packages and rinse. Combine water, bay leaf, onion, salt and dill stems and bring to the boiling point. Simmer for 30

60   FISH AND SHELLFISH

minutes, then bring back to the boiling point and drop lobster tails into the broth. Bring back to a full boil, then lower heat and poach for 10–15 minutes, depending on size of lobster tails. Remove from broth and let cool. Save broth. Cut each tail in half lengthwise through the back and remove meat in one piece. Cut into cubes. Each half tail will give about 3–4 pieces. Place in a bowl and cover with some of the broth. Chill.

Cut a slice off the end of a grapefruit, then cut off 3 ¾-inch slices. Trim off the rind with scissors or a sharp knife. Repeat with second grapefruit. Wrap grapefruit slices in waxed paper with a piece of paper between the slices. Chill.

Put mayonnaise in blender and gradually add the dill leaves. Blend until chopped fine. Chill.

When ready to serve, drain lobster pieces and shake them well to dry. Add dill mayonnaise. Divide between the grapefruit socles.

6 SERVINGS

HERRING SALAD

This salad, known as Salade de Hareng, Sill Salad, Rossolye, Herings Salat and so on, is known from the North Cape to the Alps and from the Atlantic to the Urals, wherever herring is a staple food. It is composed of diced cooked meat, diced cooked potatoes, diced raw apples, minced filets of herring and various additions such as minced pickles, chopped eggs, and in the eastern parts of Europe, diced beets.

Recipes a hundred years ago describe a "fine" herring salad made without potatoes and more meat, while some modern recipes omit the meat.

Roast veal was the most commonly used leftover meat, simply because the large leg of veal was standard holiday or Sunday roast and herring salad was the ideal way to use up all scraps. The days of the large veal roast are over, so boiled beef, roast pork, tongue and ham are substituted.

The following recipe offers an American version, using dark turkey meat:

1 turkey hindquarter, about 2 pounds cooked and diced (about 2 cups)

3 potatoes, about 1 pound cooked and diced (about 1½ cups)

2 large apples, peeled, cored and diced (about 1½ cups)

1 can (8½ ounces) julienne cut red beets, minced (about ½ cup)

3–4 small pickles, minced or 1 large pickle, minced, (about ½ cup)

2 tablespoons capers

2 hard cooked eggs, chopped

1 8-ounce jar of herring tidbits or use 4 filets of herring, Matjes or Schmaltz, minced very fine.

Cook the turkey hindquarter in stock as described in Hot Weather Turkey (p. 94), or use some of the dark meat from the Hot Weather Turkey. Remove meat from skin and bones and dice. Combine with all other ingredients and mix well. Then prepare the following dressing.

DRESSING:

½ cup oil

1 tablespoon wine vinegar

2 tablespoons red wine

1 bouillon cube

3 tablespoons warm water

½ teaspoon dry mustard

Beat together oil, wine vinegar and red wine. Add bouillon cube to water and dissolve. Add mustard, blend, then add to oil and vinegar. Spoon the dressing over the salad mixture, blending it in. The ingredients should be coated, but there should not be any liquid.

Though the various recipes may vary in special additions or omissions, they all agree on one thing: This salad needs aging for at least 12 hours, preferably 24. So prepare well ahead of time for the next smorgasbord, of which this is a mainstay.

Traditional garnishings: sliced red beets, pickles, chopped egg whites and yolks or sliced eggs.

MAKES 2 QUARTS PLUS

HERRING TIDBITS IN ENDIVE LEAVES

2 jars herring tidbits, cream style   *8 large Belgian endive leaves, or*
   (8 ounces each)   *use tender romaine lettuce*
1 can water chestnuts (8 ounces)   *leaves*
6 hard cooked egg whites   *Strips of pimientos*

D R E S S I N G :
    5 tablespoons oil   *1 teaspoon salt*
    2 tablespoons lemon juice   *½ teaspoon pepper*
    6 hard cooked egg yolks

Drain tidbits and rinse off the cream sauce. Pat dry. Chop coarsely. Chop water chestnuts and egg whites. Combine. Beat together all dressing ingredients and mix with the herring–waterchestnut–egg white mixture. Fill endive leaves and garnish with strips of pimientos.

8 SERVINGS

MARINATED MACKEREL FILETS

8 mackerel filets	1 rib celery with tops, chopped
½ cup lemon juice	5 stems parsley
1½ cups water	3 whole cloves
1 teaspoon salt	5 whole peppercorns
1 small onion, sliced	¾ cup white wine
½ carrot, sliced	

Wash fish filets, arrange in a glass bowl and pour lemon juice over all. Combine water, salt, the vegetables, parsley, cloves and peppercorns and bring to the boiling point. Simmer for 30 minutes.

Heat oven to 400° F. Add white wine to the vegetable broth and bring back to the boiling point. Arrange fish filets in a baking dish in one layer, skin side down. Strain broth over fish and bake for 15 minutes. Remove from oven; cool, then chill. Serve fish filets arranged on a round platter in a starfish pattern. Decorate the filets with dabs of Tartar Sauce and fill space between the filets with a few sliced olives, green or black, sliced mixed pickles and sliced gherkins.

8 SERVINGS

TARTAR SAUCE:

1½ cups mayonnaise	1 gherkin
2 sprigs parsley	3–4 olives, pitted
1 slice onion	1 tablespoon capers, drained

To the blender add mayonnaise, parsley and slice of onion. Chop, then gradually add sliced gherkin, olives and capers, letting blender run just long enough to chop each addition. Place in a bowl and chill.

MAKES ABOUT 2 CUPS

MEAT AND POULTRY

CORNED BEEF MOUSSE

1 can corned beef (12 ounces)
1 can onion soup (10½ ounces)
¼ cup red wine
3 envelopes plain gelatin
3 egg yolks

1 teaspoon Worcestershire sauce
¾ cup mayonnaise
½ cup heavy cream
3 egg whites

Crumble corned beef into a bowl. Drain some of the liquid from the onion soup into a small saucepan; add the remaining soup to the corned beef. Add red wine. Sprinkle gelatin over liquid in the saucepan and heat gently, stirring constantly, until gelatin dissolves. Add to the corned beef.

Put egg yolks into a blender and beat. Gradually add corned beef mixture and purée. Add Worcestershire sauce and mayonnaise; beat, and blend in the cream. Pour into a bowl. Beat egg whites until stiff, then fold them into the corned beef purée. Put into a 6-cup ring mold, chill to set and unmold on a platter. Fill center with cole slaw. Or use 6 individual molds, or divide between 8 molds and set them around a platter with cole slaw. If blender is too full to hold the whole quantity, beat 2 eggs, use half the corned beef mixture and half the mayonnaise and cream and repeat. Then combine both in a bowl and after beating the egg whites beat mixture before folding in egg whites.

6–8 SERVINGS

BLOODY MARY MEAT LOAF

1 pound ground chuck
1 cup Half & Half cream
2 eggs
2 tablespoons dry instant minced onion
1 teaspoon salt

½ teaspoon pepper
2 tablespoons tomato catsup
1 teaspoon Worcestershire sauce
½ teaspoon dry basil
1 cup fine dry bread crumbs

ASPIC:

1 can V-8 juice (12 ounces)
½ cup water
2 envelopes plain gelatin
4 ounces gin or vodka

Heat oven to 350° F. Put meat into a large bowl. To the cup of Half & Half add eggs, onion, salt, pepper, catsup, Worcestershire sauce and basil. Beat until well blended. Add bread crumbs, mix, and let stand for a minute or so to moisten well. Then add to meat, and using hands, blend the bread-crumb mixture into the meat. Put into a bread pan (9½ x 4½ x 2½) and bake for 1 hour at 350° F. When done, remove pan from oven and place upside down on a cake rack over a cookie sheet to drain off fat. Let stand to cool, then remove from pan. Wash pan and dry.

Put ½ cup water into a small saucepan and sprinkle the 2 envelopes gelatin over the water. Stir gently, then heat over low flame to dissolve gelatin. Add gelatin to V-8 juice; add gin. Pour about ¼ cup or more into clean meat loaf pan, enough to cover bottom about ½ inch deep. Place in refrigerator to chill and set. Do not chill remaining liquid. When liquid in pan is well set, place meat loaf back into pan and pour remaining liquid over it. Chill at least overnight.

To unmold, loosen edges, dip or stand in warm water, count to 10 and reverse on a service platter. If a garnish is desired such as sliced olives or peeled lemon slices, dissolve 2 teaspoons gelatin in ¼ cup water, add lemon juice, chill but keep liquid. Dip garnishes in liquid and arrange on top of Bloody Mary Meat Loaf.

6–8 SERVINGS

HIDDEN BUTTON MEATBALLS

2 cups beef chuck, ground
¾ cup chopped onion
1 can anchovy fillets, drained
4 slices white bread, trimmed

4 tablespoons Half & Half or
light cream
4 eggs
1 teaspoon salt
½ teaspoon pepper

BROTH:

8 cups water
1 onion, cut in half
1 bay leaf
1 teaspoon salt

1 can pickled mushrooms (3¾ ounces)

Grind store-ground meat with onions and drained anchovies using a coarse blade. Moisten trimmed bread with cream, and crumble. Add to meat, together with eggs and salt and pepper. Mix well with ground meat, then put the whole once more through the meat grinder, this time using the finest blade. The finer the mixture is ground, the lighter the meatballs will be. Fill a roasting pan or similar vessel with water (approximately 8 cups) or about ⅔ full. Add onion, bay leaf and salt and gently boil for 20 minutes.

Divide meat mixture into 12 or 13 even portions. Press a pickled mushroom into the center and shape into balls. When all are done, lower the heat under the boiling water to a simmer and drop meatballs into it. Lower and raise the heat as needed; watch carefully so that the water does not boil or meatballs will break. Simmer for approximately 20 minutes; meatballs will come to the surface when done. With a slotted spoon remove meatballs from liquid and let cool. Strain liquid. Put meatballs in a bowl, pour strained liquid over them and chill. Remove fat from chilled meatballs; drain off liquid and reserve 5 cups. Put meatballs on a flat surface to drain further. Chill.

SAUCE:

4 tablespoons butter	*Few drops yellow food coloring*
4 tablespoons flour	*Juice of 2 lemons*
2 cups cooking liquid	*4–5 teaspoons drained capers*

GELATIN:

1 cup liquid
1 teaspoon plain gelatin
2 teaspoons cornstarch

GARNISH:

Capers

Over low heat melt butter, add flour, and when well blended add the 2 cups of cooking liquid, stirring constantly; cook until sauce is thickened. Simmer for 5 minutes.

Put some water into a tablespoon and add a few drops of yellow food coloring. Very carefully add this diluted coloring to the sauce until it is a dark ivory color. Do not try to do this from the coloring bottle. (One always pours too much.) Season sauce with the juice of the 2 lemons and add the capers. Bring once more to the boiling point, then cool and chill.

Put the 1 cup of cooking liquid into a small saucepan, sprinkle gelatin over it and add cornstarch. Stir constantly gradually bring to the boiling point, and add this to the yellow sauce.

Arrange meatballs on a service platter, making either 3 pyramids of 4 balls each or make one large pyramid, starting with 5, then 4, then 3, then 1, for a total of 13. Spoon the combined sauces over the meatballs, coating them well on all sides. Repeat twice, chilling in the meantime. After they are coated, sprinkle some capers around the pyramids. To the leftover coating sauces add some of the cooking liquid (about 2 cups), just enough to thin the sauce to a consistency of mayonnaise. Add some capers and serve on the side.

6–8 SERVINGS

HAM IN ASPIC

1 canned (approximately 2
    pounds) ham (18–20
    slices)
2 cans clear chicken broth
1 cup water

2½ envelopes plain gelatin (2½
    tablespoons)
1 loaf pan (9 X 5 X 2½)
½ hard cooked egg
1 package frozen Chinese pea
    pods

Chill ham in can overnight. Combine chicken broth and water. Sprinkle gelatin over 1 cup chicken broth, then heat to dissolve. Add this gelatin liquid to the rest of the chicken broth and water. Chill in refrigerator until it begins to jell slightly, but is not syrupy.

Cook pea pods in small amount of salted water until just blanched and still very crisp. Drain and chill. Put loaf pan in freezer or refrigerator. When chicken broth liquid begins to jell, set pan in a pan with crushed ice. Turn pan so that small side faces you. Put a small amount of gelatin liquid in pan, just enough for a thin layer, place the hard cooked egg half against the small side of the pan farthest away. Make a decorative pattern with the pea pods over the layer of gelatin, arranging them along the rim and in the middle. Carefully spoon more liquid over the pea pods to set them.

Open can of ham, scrape off all jelly and discard. Cut a thin slice from the wide side and set aside for other purposes, then slice into 18 or 20 slices, again setting aside the small end slice. When the jelly coating the pea pods is almost set, arrange ham slices in mold, leaning them against the egg half on a slant. Add some more of the gelatin liquid and slide some pea pods between the ham slices and along the wall. Fill up with remaining gelatin liquid. Let stand to set, then place in refrigerator overnight.

To unmold, loosen the gelatin all around the edges. Hold mold in a vessel filled with warm water (or fill the sink) all the way to the brim. Count to ten. Wipe mold dry. Invert on a service platter. Remove egg half and gelatin from first slice. The ham slices will now slant backward. If any repairs on the decorations are needed, melt the gelatin removed from first slice. Chill and coat any defects.

8–10 SERVINGS OR MORE FOR BUFFET

STUFFED TONGUE

1 tongue (3½–4½ pounds)	*½ an onion*
1 bay leaf	*A few whole cloves*
1 teaspoon whole peppercorns	*Water*

STUFFING:

1 cup port wine	*½ cup water*
4 ounces sour cream	*1 pound seedless fresh grapes*
3 envelopes plain gelatin	

DECORATION:

½ cup water	*½ cup port wine*
3 teaspoons cornstarch	*Reserved whole grapes*
1 envelope plain gelatin	

In a large pot, cover tongue with water, add onion, bay leaf, peppercorns and cloves and bring to the boiling point. Simmer for about 2½–3 hours, depending on size of tongue. Start testing after 2 hours by piercing tip of tongue with a fork.

When done, remove tongue from broth and let cool enough to handle. Remove skin and cut off from the underside all the gristle, fat, and tendons to have an even cut. From the cut-off parts salvage all pieces of good meat. (It is quite a bit.) From the whole tongue cut off the tip, about 2–2½ inches long, the whole thin part. Then cut off the hump of the tongue to have a boxlike piece of meat. Put the large tongue piece and all cut-off meat, including scraps, into a bowl, strain over enough cooking liquid to cover and set aside to chill overnight. Put all the cut-off meat into a blender, add 1 cup port wine and purée. Remove to a bowl; add sour cream. Sprinkle the 3 envelopes gelatin over ½ cup water and gently heat to dissolve. Add to the meat purée.

Cut enough grapes in half to have about 2 cups. Reserve the remaining grapes for decoration. Add the cut grapes to the meat purée and mix.

Make a slit in the tongue block in the middle to about ¾ inch from the bottom and leave at least ½ inch on the side walls.

Line a bread pan, large enough to fit the tongue (about 9½ x 5½ x 2½) with aluminum foil, leaving a good amount of foil to hang over the sides to facilitate removing later on. Set the tongue in the lined bread pan. Fill the slit tongue with the meat purée–grape mixture, pushing down, then fill in around the tongue, but not over it. Set aside to chill. When tongue filling is set, combine ½ cup water with the 3 teaspoons cornstarch and sprinkle gelatin over it. Heat gently to the boiling point until liquid is clear, then add port wine. Scatter remaining grapes over the surface of the tongue, cut some in half to make a pattern, if desired, and gently spoon some of the liquid over the whole. Repeat and make sure all grapes are coated. If liquid gets too solid, reheat gently and continue coating. Chill to set. To unmold: Loosen aluminum foil, set pan in warm water, then lift out with foil and peel off the foil. Serve tongue on a platter; cut tongue first through the middle, then from there to both sides so as to have meat and fillings on all servings. If there is any leftover filling or tongue, chop meat, reheat and remold in individual molds.

8–10 SERVINGS

SPICED HAM

*4–5 pounds fresh ham, weighed
with bone in, boned and
rolled*

MARINADE:

2–3 cups red wine
¾ cup tarragon vinegar
*1 teaspoon each of ground ginger,
ground cloves, ground allspice, ground pepper, dry
tarragon*

*3 tablespoons minced instant
onion*
*2 tablespoons juniper berries,
crushed*
4–5 bay leaves
*Peel of 1 lemon (cut off with
potato peeler)*

FOR ROASTING:

*3 tablespoons bacon drippings or
oil*
Water

GARNISH:

Red wine
Plain gelatin

Ask butcher when boning ham to cut off skin and trim off fat before rolling. Combine in a bowl some of the wine, vinegar, spices, onions, juniper berries, bay leaves, lemon peel and mix. Place ham in a tight fitting stainless steel or earthenware vessel and pour the marinade over it. Then add enough wine to cover half the ham. Let stand for 2 days, turning once a day.

Remove ham from marinade; strain marinade.

Heat oven to 325° F. Heat bacon drippings or oil in a Dutch oven or casserole with a cover and brown ham on all sides. Add equal parts of strained marinade and water to reach to one half of ham's thickness. Cover and bake for 1½ hours, then uncover, insert meat thermometer and finish baking until thermometer reads 185° F. about ½ hour more.

Remove ham from baking vessel, place in a bowl, strain baking liquid over it, and add enough red wine to cover ham about ¾. Cover and chill. Remove fat accumulated on top and take ham out. Wipe fat off ham. Strain liquid in bowl and measure. For each 2 cups liquid dissolve 1 envelope plain gelatin. Pour into a square mold, chill to set and use to garnish sliced ham. Or chill until creamy, then spoon over sliced ham.

10–12 SERVINGS

PRUNED LOIN OF PORK

4–5 pounds loin of pork	*½ teaspoon each of ground cinna-*
2–3 cans prune juice	*mon, ground cloves,*
2–3 cans water	*ground nutmeg*
1 teaspoon each ground allspice	*2 teaspoons salt*
and ground ginger	*8 peppercorns*
	Heat oven to 325° F.

GARNISH:

Red wine
1 envelope plain gelatin

The pork loin can be in one or two pieces, depending on vessel selected. Place meat in a casserole with cover, as small as possible to accommodate the meat piece. Add enough prune juice and water in even proportions to cover the meat up to ¾ thickness. Add all spices. Cover and bake for a total of 2–3 hours depending on weight and thickness. Turn meat after the first hour, cover, bake another hour, turn again and insert meat thermometer. Continue baking uncovered until internal temperature reads 185° F.

Remove meat from casserole and place in a glass or stainless steel vessel. Strain liquid from the casserole over the meat. Chill until fat is solidified, preferably overnight. Remove fat and discard.

The liquid around the meat should be slightly solidified. Transfer meat and liquid to a saucepan and heat just enough to liquify jelly. Remove meat from liquid. Measure liquid and add enough red wine to make 2 cups. Pour ½ cup into a small saucepan, sprinkle with gelatin and heat gently, stirring constantly until gelatin is dissolved. Combine with other liquid and set aside to chill to a creamy consistency.

Remove meat from bones and slice. Arrange slices on a platter and spoon creamy liquid between and over the slices. Chill before serving.

8–12 SERVINGS

POTTED BEEF

3–4 pounds boneless chuck roast, tied

MARINADE:

3 tablespoons instant onion
1 teaspoon each of ground cinnamon, ground allspice,

ground cloves, salt and pepper
½ cup water
Vinegar to cover

FOR ROAST:

1 large onion, sliced
¾ cup marinade
2 cups water
1 cup chopped carrots

1 cup chopped parsnips
½ cup butter or margarine
¼ cup marinade
½ cup water

Port wine
2 envelopes plain gelatin

To marinate meat put it in a stainless steel or earthenware vessel, add the instant onion, spices, water and vinegar, and let stand in refrigerator overnight. The next day take out meat and strain marinade. Heat oven to 375° F. Place roast in a Dutch oven or casserole with a cover. Arrange sliced onion on top of meat, then add the ¾ cup marinade and 2 cups water. Cover and roast for 1½ hours. In the meantime combine chopped carrots, chopped parsnips and butter in a frying pan and sauté until lightly browned; add ¼ cup marinade and ½ cup water, simmer until vegetables are very soft, and reduce liquid until they have a spreadable consistency. After 1½ hours of roasting, spread the vegetables over top of roast, check on the liquid and add marinade and water as needed. Cover again and roast for another hour, then test for doneness. Cooking time varies from 2½–3 hours depending on grade of meat.

Remove meat from roaster, put in a bowl, pour pan drippings over meat and chill. Remove fat, wipe meat, wrap and chill. Heat pan drippings and strain through a fine sieve. Measure and add enough port wine to make 3½ cups. Put ½ cup of this liquid in a small saucepan, sprinkle gelatin over it and heat gently, stirring constantly, until gelatin is dissolved. Pour into a square pan and chill to set.

To serve, slice meat and garnish with large cubes of the port wine-gelatin from the pan.

8 SERVINGS

BOILED BEEF MOLDED

2–3 *pounds chuck steaks*
6 *cups water*
1 *onion stuck with a clove*
Parsley stems and celery tops,
    about 2 cups
1 *bay leaf*

2 *teaspoons salt*
1 *teaspoon pepper*
3 *envelopes plain gelatin*
1 *teaspoon Worcestershire sauce*
1 *package frozen peas and onions*
    (10 *ounces*)

DRESSING:

8 *ounces* (1 *cup*) *cottage cheese*
3 *tablespoons milk*

1 *jar prepared horseradish* (6
    ounces)
½ *cup sour cream*

If possible cut bones from meat. Combine bones, water, onion, parsley, celery, bay leaf, salt and pepper in a large saucepan and simmer for ¾–1 hour. Put meat into another saucepan and strain the boiling liquid over it, discarding vegetables and seasonings; simmer for about 30 minutes, depending on thickness of cut, or until meat is soft.

Strain liquid and measure (there should be about 5 cups). Add Worcestershire sauce. Measure 1 cup into a small saucepan, sprinkle gelatin on top and heat gently, stirring constantly until gelatin is dissolved. Add to other liquid and taste for seasoning.

When meat is cool enough to handle trim off gristle and cut meat into small cubes. Cook peas and onions according to directions on package. Add to meat. Put some of the gelatin liquid over meat and vegetables and pour remaining into a loaf pan. Chill until it begins to set, then add the meat–vegetable–liquid mixture. This way meat and vegetables will be held in suspension and stay in the middle of the mold. Chill overnight. To unmold, set the mold into a pan of warm water, count to ten, and reverse onto a platter.

For the dressing, combine cottage cheese and milk in a blender, and beat until smooth.

Drain horseradish and press dry; add to blender and mix. Add sour cream and blend for just 1 second. Taste for seasonings and add salt as needed.

6–8 SERVINGS

ROAST FILET OF BEEF

1 beef filet (tenderloin), 6–7 pounds
4 strips bacon

If you are courageous buy the beef tenderloin "as is" with all the fat on. Just start peeling off the layers of fat, trim off the fat on the sides and remove the tendons that run along the sides of the filet. (Save that strip of meat, it is good ground and also as a goulash.) Dig in at the "head," the thickest part, and don't be discouraged by the mountain of fat that is removed. A 6–7 pound filet "as is" trims down to about 3½–4 pounds, but that is enough for 8–10 people, even if the filet is the only meat served.

The classical way to prepare the filet for roasting is to lard it with "smoked bacon"; a simpler way is to put 4 strips of bacon over the length of the filet. Roast at 375°–400° F. for 40 minutes for rare. Place meat in a preheated oven. Remove bacon strips after 30 minutes roasting time.

Take pan with meat from the oven and let cool, then chill. Slice rather thin when cold.

Serve with Cumberland sauce.

Cumberland Sauce

> *1 orange peel*
> *2 tablespoons dry mustard*
> *4 tablespoons red wine*
> *1 jar currant jelly (10 ounces)*

With a potato peeler remove skin from orange; do not press hard, just the yellow part is needed, not the white skin underneath. With a pair of scissors snip this peel very fine.

Mix mustard and red wine to a paste. With a fork beat currant jelly, add orange peel snippings and mustard paste and blend.

Chill before serving.

8–10 SERVINGS

LEG OF LAMB THAT IS "ANOTHER ANIMAL"

This is an old recipe of my mother's based on a method of preserving meat before refrigeration. The lamb was covered with milk and buttermilk and stored in the springhouse until ready to use. We made this recipe for Jane Nickerson and she described it in her *New York Times* column April 8, 1953. If you don't like cold lamb, just try this. As Jane said, "The meat, on biting into, tasted like lamb but on swallowing left an after flavor that was tangy, almost gamelike."

> *1 leg of lamb, 4–5 pounds before*   *5 bacon strips*
>   *boning*   *1 tablespoon juniper berries,*
> *1 quart buttermilk*   *slightly crushed*
> *1–2 quarts sweet milk*   *1 cup white wine*

Have butcher bone and roll leg of lamb and ask him to remove all fat, or at least as much as possible. If you don't trust him, untie leg of lamb, check and trim it yourself and retie. Place leg of lamb in a stainless steel or eathenware bowl and cover with buttermilk and milk, as much as needed. Let stand in the refrigerator for a week, turning meat once a day.

Heat oven to 375° F. Remove meat from milk, wipe dry, discard milk. Place meat in roasting pan, cover with bacon strips, add wine and juniper berries and insert meat thermometer. Roast for 2–2½ hours until meat thermometer indicates 175° F. Lamb will be slightly underdone.

Remove meat from pan, cool, then cover and chill. Pour pan drippings in bowl and chill. Degrease. The liquid should be creamy or jelled. Slice meat and spoon pan-dripping jelly over it. If desired serve with minted pineapple or peaches.

Minted Pineapple or Peaches
Canned pineapple chunks or peach halves (16 ounces)
Water
1 envelope plain gelatin
1 jar minted apple jelly

Drain liquid from fruits; measure and add enough water to make 1½ cups. Put ½ cup in small saucepan, sprinkle with gelatin and stir constantly, disolving gelatin. Add mint jelly and melt. Combine with remaining liquid and fruits. Put in a fancy mold or in a square pan. Chill until set. Arrange sliced meat around fancy mold or cut jellied fruits into squares and arrange around sliced meat.

8–10 SERVINGS

VEAL ROAST

2½–3 pounds boneless veal
shoulder, rolled
1 can anchovy fillets
3 strips bacon

1 cup white wine
More white wine, for after
roasting
1 envelope plain gelatin

APPLE MAYONNAISE DRESSING:

3–4 tart apples
1 cup white wine
1 envelope plain gelatin

2 limes
1 teaspoon dry mustard
½ cup mayonnaise

Heat oven to 375° F. Wipe meat and with a sharp knife cut holes into the upper part of the roll. Insert a fillet of anchovy into the holes, pressing down hard with fingers. Use up all fillets and dribble oil over the surface. Cover with bacon strips, set in a small roasting pan and add the wine. Insert meat thermometer. Roast for 1½–2 hours; remove strips of bacon after first hour, until internal temperature reaches just below 180° F.

Remove from pan, put upside down in a pan that is just large enough to hold the roast; add pan drippings and fill up with enough white wine to cover roast almost completely.

Set aside to chill. Remove fat collected on top. Remove roast and wipe off fat. Measure liquid in pan. For each 1½ cups used sprinkle 1 envelope gelatin over part of the liquid and heat gently stirring constantly, until gelatin is dissolved.

Cut strings from meat and slice thin. Pour some of the liquid back into the loaf pan and arrange sliced meat in the pan, the slices overlapping. Pour the remaining liquid over the slices and chill until set. Unmold by setting the pan in warm water and counting to ten, then reverse over a service platter. Make sure to remove the first slice from mold at the right end to show overlapping slices.

Serve with Apple Mayonnaise Dressing: Peel and core apples, cut in quarters, add white wine and simmer until apples are very soft. Remove some of the liquid into a small saucepan, sprinkle with gelatin, heat gently, stirring constantly, until gelatin is dissolved; add to apples, add the juice of the 2 limes and the dry mustard. Pour into blender and blend until light and fluffy. Put in a bowl and chill until it begins to thicken, then add the ½ cup mayonnaise. Chill before serving.

6–8 SERVINGS

ROLLED BREAST OF VEAL

*1 breast of veal, 3½–4½
pounds.*

STOCK:

Bones from breast of veal	*2 teaspoons peppercorns*
1 large onion, quartered	*1 large bay leaf*
¾ cup celery tops	*Water*

FILLING:

1½ tablespoons butter or	*1 egg*
margarine	*½ cup chopped parsley*
¾ cup chopped onion	*¼ teaspoon nutmeg*
3 slices white bread, trimmed	*1 teaspoon salt*
¾ cup milk	*½ teaspoon pepper*
¾ pound chopped beef chuck	*4 tablespoons margarine or oil for*
¼ pound sausage meat	*browning*

FINALE:

1 envelope plain gelatin

Have butcher bone breast of veal or do it yourself. Put bones in a pot, add quartered onion, celery tops, peppercorns and bay leaf, and enough water to cover. Simmer for ¾ hour covered; then raise the heat and boil for another half hour. Strain stock and measure. If it is more than 4½ cups boil some more to concentrate. Discard bones and vegetables.

While stock is simmering, prepare the filling: Melt butter, add onions and sauté until they are transparent but do not brown (about 5–10 minutes). Let cool in pan.

Put bread slices in a large bowl. Add the milk. Mash with a fork until milk is absorbed. Add chopped beef, sausage meat, egg, parsley, nutmeg, salt and pepper and finally the cooled onions. Mix the whole together until it is well blended. Your hands are the best tool.

Heat oven to 350° F. Wipe breast of veal with a damp cloth to remove all bone splinters that might adhere. Spread the filling over it evenly. Roll up jelly-roll fashion and tie first in the middle, then on both ends. In a large frying pan melt the margarine or oil and brown the veal roll on all sides, but do not let burn. Keep turning. Transfer to a roasting pan, casserole or Dutch oven (all with cover), pour some of the prepared stock into the frying pan, heat to loosen all brown particles, then pour over meat roll. Reserve ½ cup of stock and pour the remaining over the meat roll. Cover and roast in a 350° F. oven for a total of 2½ hours. After 1 hour, turn the roll; cover. After second hour, turn once more, uncover and cook the remaining half hour basting once or twice. Remove meat roll from roasting pan and place in a loaf pan. Strain the cooking liquid. Sprinkle 1 envelope of gelatin over the reserved ½ cup of stock and heat gently to dissolve gelatin. Add this to the cooking liquid, then pour the whole over the meat roll in the loaf pan. If it is too much liquid, pour excess into a small bowl. Cover with plastic wrap and chill everything overnight.

Scrape and wipe fat off the meat roll. Remove from loaf pan, cut ties and discard. The liquid in the pan should be jelled, if not reheat and add 1 envelope of plain gelatin for every 2 cups liquid. To serve, slice roll and garnish with chopped jelled liquid.

6–8 SERVINGS

PICKLE BOATS

This is a "quickie delicatessen" dish.

Large delicatessen chains usually have a so-called "meat salad," made from the ends of ham, corned beef, bolognas, soft salamis, mortadellas or any other sausage except hard salami and liverwurst. These ends are cut julienne style, a few finely cut pickles or gherkins are added, and the whole mixed with mayonnaise. If you cannot buy this salad, make it yourself.

1 pound assorted cold cuts, such as ham, bologna, cooked salami and the like	*Mayonnaise*
	4 large pickles, such as kosher dills
8 small gherkins or other pickles	*Strips of pimientos for garnish*

Cut the ham and cold cuts into small strips; dice or cut into strips the gherkins or pickles. Add enough mayonnaise to bind. Chill.

Cut large pickles in half lengthwise and scoop out seeds. Chill. Fill pickle shells with meat salad. Smooth surface and coat with mayonnaise. Garnish with pimiento strips.

8 SERVINGS

GLAZED CORNISH HENS

2 Cornish hens
5 tablespoons orange marma-
    lade (preferably the clear
    type)

1½ tablespoons dry mustard
1 orange, quartered
½ cup orange juice

GLAZE:

1 cup baking liquid
1 envelope plain gelatin
3 teaspoons cornstarch

Preheat oven to 350° F. Using poultry shears and knife, cut hens in half. Wash and pat dry. Blend marmalade and mustard. Arrange the 4 halves in a roasting pan and stick a quarter of the orange under each. Brush the hens heavily with the marmalade–mustard mixture and make sure each part is well covered. Add orange juice. Cover lightly with aluminum foil and bake for ¾ hour then remove foil and bake uncovered for ½ hour more. Remove from oven, cool slightly, then transfer the halves with their orange quarters to a serving platter. Strain baking liquid and let cool; if there is less than a cup, add orange juice. Mix with gelatin and cornstarch and cook until gelatin is dissolved and it is clear. Spoon over hens once. Then chill hens. After about 2 hours give them another coat. If coating has set, reheat gently. Repeat once more and chill hens. Chop and use as garnish any leftover coating.

4 SERVINGS

CHICKEN BREAST IN ASPIC

3 broilers or	*½ onion stuck with a clove*
3 whole chicken breasts and 2	*1 bay leaf*
pounds chicken backs	*1 tablespoon salt*
1 cup celery tops	*8 cups water*
1 carrot	

M O L D :

1 13 X 9 X 2-pan lined with	*2 raw egg whites and egg shell*
aluminum foil	*Pimientos, olives, pickles, water-*
Water	*cress*
5 envelopes of plain gelatin	

If broilers are used remove wings and legs and cut off backs. Put wings and backs with gizzards, neck and heart with celery, carrot, onion and seasonings in a large pot, add water, and bring to the boiling point. Simmer for ¾–1 hour. (Reserve legs for another meal.) If breast and backs are used simmer backs and vegetables. After stock has cooked add the breasts and simmer for 20 minutes; remove and cool. Carefully remove meat in one piece from bones and skin. Put in a bowl and cover with some of the simmering broth. Cool and chill. Return breastbones and skin to simmering broth, add 2–3 cups water and continue simmering for another 30 minutes to an hour. Strain, discard bones and vegetables and cool broth. Chill till next day. The broth should be jelled. Remove all fat and wipe all specks of fat off with paper towels. Melt the jelled broth and measure. Add enough water to make 10 cups. For each 2 cups sprinkle 1 envelope gelatin over the liquid. Beat the egg whites lightly and add to the broth together with the crumbled shells. Beat well and bring to the boiling point. When foaming, turn off heat and let stand for a few minutes, then strain through a damp heavy cloth. Do not disturb, it has to run clear. (If it is not clear the cloth is not heavy enough. Strain again.) Chill for an hour or so. Set the aluminum lined pan in a larger pan with crushed ice. The gelatin broth should still be liquid; pour a small amount into the pan and let set. Place breasts of chicken on top, smooth side up, spacing them evenly. Add more liquid but do not cover chicken breasts yet. Let them set a bit, then decorate as desired, each breast in a fancy pattern. Gradually fill the pan with the still liquid broth. Spoon a bit over the decorations to make this a heavier coating. Let stand until fairly set, then chill overnight. To serve, carefully lift the chicken breast from the pan with the aluminum foil. Cut neatly around each breast and place on a service platter. Chop leftover aspic and arrange on platter as a decoration or make into snow by pressing it through a sieve. Garnish with pimientos, pickles, olives or watercress.

6 SERVINGS

BAKED CHICKEN LIVER PUDDING

1 pound chicken livers, approximately	*2 tablespoons Parmesan cheese*
4 slices white bread, untrimmed	*1 teaspoon salt*
¼ cup milk	*½ teaspoon pepper*
4 slices bacon	*4 egg yolks*
5–6 scallions, white part only	*4 egg whites*

Drain livers. Crumble untrimmed bread into a bowl, add milk to moisten bread. Cut up bacon and in a frying pan over low heat fry gently without browning. Chop scallions and add to bacon. Sauté until limp. Add moistened bread, cheese, salt and pepper and remove from heat. Put egg yolks in blender and beat; gradually add chicken livers and purée. Then add bacon–bread–scallion mixture gradually and blend until smooth. Pour into a bowl, beat egg whites until stiff and gently fold into the liver purée. Butter a 6-cup, or larger, loaf pan. Pour the liver mixture into it, set into a larger pan filled with water and bake in a 375° F. oven for 1 hour or until a knife inserted comes out clean. For small molds the baking time is reduced to about ¾ hour. After baking, cool, then chill, then unmold.

6–8 SERVINGS

CHICKEN PIE

1 chicken, broiler or fryer, 2½–3
    pounds
6 cups water or more
2 tablespoons dehydrated soup
    greens
1 tablespoon dehydrated onion
3 tomatoes

1 tablespoon salt
2 tablespoons vinegar
1 can small artichoke hearts (7
    ounces)
1 can water chestnuts (8 ounces)
3 envelopes plain gelatin

GARNISH:
2 hard cooked eggs, sliced

Disjoint chicken into legs and breast part. Put backs, wings, neck and gizzard with the water into a 3-quart saucepan and add soup greens, onion, tomatoes and salt. Simmer for 45 minutes to 1 hour. Add vinegar and chicken breast and legs. Simmer breast for about 15–18 minutes and legs for 25 minutes. Remove both and cool. Keep broth simmering. Remove meat from breast and legs and return bones and skin to broth. Simmer for another 15 minutes, then strain broth. Add meat to broth and chill. Next day remove all fat from stock. Reheat enough to melt and remove meat. Cut meat into bite-sized pieces. Drain artichokes and cut in quarters. Drain water chestnuts and slice. Mix with chicken pieces. Arrange this mixture in a 9- or 10-inch pie pan. Measure 1 cup from stock, put in a small saucepan, sprinkle gelatin over it and heat gently to dissolve gelatin. Add this to 2 more cups of stock, stir and taste for seasoning. Pour as much of this liquid over the meat mixture in pie pan as needed to fill pan and pour remaining liquid into a bowl. There should be about 1½ cups left; if not, because a larger pie pan has been used, dissolve 1 more envelope gelatin in 1 cup of stock and add to the remainder. When liquids are set in pie pan and bowl, chop the gelatin in the bowl very fine or rub through a food mill or coarse sieve to make snow. Take ½ cup of this gelatin and melt. Reserve 3 tablespoons and mix the remaining liquid with the snow. Spread over chicken pie like a crust. Dip egg slices in reserved 3 tablespoons gelatin liquid and arrange in a wreath around the pie. Chill pie before serving. From the pie dish, cut in wedges like a regular pie. If desired, serve mayonnaise on the side.

6–8 SERVINGS

DOUBLE MOLD BREAST OF CHICKEN OVER RICE AND PEA SALAD

Select 2 molds; 1 holding 3–4 cups, the other, larger and wider, holding 6–7 cups.

2 broilers, 2½–3 pounds	*7 cups water*
1 pound chicken backs	*1 tablespoon salt*
3 tablespoons dry soup greens or	*1 teaspoon pepper*
Stems of parsley, celery leaves, 1	*1 bay leaf*
onion	*Juice of 1 lemon*

SALAD:

½ cup converted rice
Water
1 package frozen green peas (10 ounces)
1½ envelopes plain gelatin

ASPIC:

4 cups of liquid from chicken
3 envelopes of plain gelatin

Remove legs from broilers and use for another meal. Cut off wings and cut out backs. Put wings and backs with necks, gizzards and extra backs in a large saucepan, add soup greens and cover with water, at least 7 cups. Simmer for 1 hour. If pot is large enough, put chicken breasts into the pot and simmer for 20–25 minutes; if not, put breasts into a smaller pot and cover with some of the simmering broth. Remove breasts from broth, but continue to simmer broth for another 30 minutes. When breasts are cool enough to handle, remove meat in large pieces, pick over and save scraps. Sprinkle with lemon juice, cover and chill. Strain broth. Measure off 4 cups and put them aside to chill. This is for the coating aspic. Measure off 2 cups for peas and add enough water to make another 1½ cups. To this 1½ cups liquid add ½ cup rice and cook for 20 minutes, following instructions on package. Put the 2 cups chicken liquid for peas in a small saucepan, sprinkle with 1½ envelopes of gelatin and heat, stirring constantly, until gelatin is dissolved. Add the package of frozen peas; cook for 5–7 minutes. Combine cooked peas and liquid with cooked rice, add the chicken scraps, and place in a 3–4 cup bowl with a rounded bottom. Cool, then chill. When set, about 4–6 hours, loosen around the edges, dip in warm water and reverse on a plate. Then reverse again into a larger bowl, which allows about a ½–¾ inch margin between the peas and rice mold and the side of the bowl. Arrange the breast of chicken around the peas and rice mold, cutting them if necessary to fit between the margin. Use ½ cup of the 4 cups liquid reserved for the coating aspic, put it in a saucepan, sprinkle with the 3 envelopes of gelatin, and heat gently, stirring constantly, until gelatin is dissolved. Add the remaining 3½ cups liquid and mix. First spoon some of the liquid over the setup in the bowl, then carefully pour it over until all is covered. Run a knife around the edge to make sure that chicken breasts do not stick to the bowl. Set to chill overnight. Chill any leftover liquid and chop and use as decoration. To unmold, set in warm water, count to ten, then reverse on a service platter.

4 SERVINGS

CHICKEN TO GNAW ON

6 *chicken legs*
½ *stick margarine*
2 *teaspoons paprika*
1 *cucumber*
1 *zucchini*

3 *carrots*
6 *scallions*
1 *bowl Russian or Roquefort*
    dressing

Preheat oven to 350° F. Remove skin from chicken legs, then cut them in half at the joint, making 12 pieces. Put them on a cookie sheet with rim. Melt margarine; when foaming stops add paprika, remove from heat and mix. Brush the chicken pieces well all over with the margarine. Place in the preheated oven and bake for 1 hour, then turn pieces, add ½ cup water, bake for 15 minutes more, then turn again and bake for another 15 minutes. Remove from oven, place chicken pieces in a bowl and pour the baking liquid over all. Chill. Peel and halve cucumber, remove seeds and cut each half through the middle, then into 6 sticks. Blanch zucchini in salted water for 1 minute, trim off ends, then cut into 6 pieces, lengthwise. Peel carrots and cut into sticks. Trim scallions. Arrange vegetables like a flower arrangement in a bowl filled with either Russian or Roquefort dressing. Place in the middle of a service bowl, arrange chicken pieces around it and serve with napkins.

6 SERVINGS

DUCK IN ASPIC

2 *ducklings, approximately 5*   *1 bay leaf*
    pounds each, thawed out,   *1 tablespoon peppercorns*
    with giblets but without   *1 tablespoon salt*
    liver   *4 cups water*
2 *medium onions, sliced*   *1 cup vinegar*
2 *carrots, sliced*   *White wine*
3 *stalks celery, with tops cut in*   *3 envelopes plain gelatin*
    pieces   *2 egg whites and shells*

GARNISH:

    2 *cans button mushrooms*
    2 *cans pimientos*

Arrange vegetables with bay leaf, pepper and salt in a roasting pan with cover. Place duckling breasts down on top of vegetables. Add water, vinegar and giblets; save liver for other purposes. Cover roaster and place in a preheated 350° F. oven. Bake covered for 30 minutes, then turn ducks and bake for another 30–45 minutes until legs are tender. Remove ducks from liquid and let cool. Strain liquid from vegetables. Chill. Skin ducks and discard skin. Take meat off legs and other bones, and cube. Remove breasts and slice. Cover and chill. Remove fat from cooking liquid using paper toweling to absorb any remaining traces of fat. Drain mushrooms and add liquid. Measure liquids and add enough white wine to have 6 cups. Place in a large saucepan, sprinkle the 3 envelopes of gelatin over it, add the slightly beaten egg whites and the shells and bring the whole to the boiling point. Simmer for about 10 minutes, set aside to cool a bit, then strain through a piece of flannel or a triple thickness of kitchen toweling. Make sure it runs clear. Select a 2-quart mold, plain or fancy, and set it on ice. Pour some of the clarified gelatin into the mold and let set. Then arrange mushrooms and pimientos in an attractive pattern over the thin layer of gelatin. Spoon in some more liquid to set the garnish. Dip the slices of breast in the gelatin liquid and arrange over the decorations, overlapping. Let set. Then fill in with the cubed meat and gently spoon gelatin over this. Wait until about to set before adding remaining liquid or the cubes will float to the top. Chill overnight. Remove from mold by holding in warm water and reversing onto a service platter.

6–8 SERVINGS

CHICKEN LIVER LOAF

½ *pound chicken livers*
1 can boned chicken or turkey (5 ounces) or ¾ cup leftover chicken or turkey
½ *stick butter*
1 cup chopped onions

2 tablespoons flour
1 cup sherry
4 egg yolks (large eggs)
2 tablespoons chopped parsley
1 teaspoon salt
½ *teaspoon pepper*

GARNISH:

4 egg whites
½ *cup water*
¼ *cup sherry*

2 teaspoons gelatin
1 teaspoon cornstarch
2 tablespoons chopped parsley

Preheat oven to 350° F. Drain chicken livers. Put boned chicken in the blender. Melt butter, add onions and sauté until they begin to get glassy. Add livers. Over low heat sauté livers until they are just done (they may show some pink in the inside). Sprinkle the flour over the whole, mix, then add sherry. Bring to the boiling point. Transfer the whole to the blender and purée. Put in a bowl, add egg yolks one at a time and mix well. Add parsley, salt and pepper. Butter a bread pan (9 x 5 x 2½) very well and pour the liver mixture into it. Place in oven and bake for 1½ hours at 350° F.

While loaf is baking wrap egg whites into aluminum foil and drop into boiling water. Let simmer for 3 minutes, then cover and let stand for 20 minutes. Remove from foil to a plate and chill.

Prepare the garnish: combine water, sherry, gelatin and cornstarch; over low heat slowly bring to the boiling point, stirring constantly. Set aside but do not chill. Test with a knife blade or skewer; if it comes out clean, loaf is done. Let cool in the pan for 15 minutes, then turn out on a service plate. While still hot, glaze with the sherry-gelatin mixture once, then sprinkle with the chopped egg whites and parsley and glaze again. Repeat once more and be sure all is covered. Set aside to cool, then chill overnight.

4–6 SERVINGS

HOT WEATHER TURKEY

I am a compulsive reader of grocery ads. Somehow they tell me more about the state of the economy than a Wall Street report and I love a bargain. So when turkey prices dropped below chicken prices I tried to figure out how to use turkey instead of chicken. Then I called my friend Jane Nickerson, food editor and columnist of the Lakeland *Florida Ledger* and other small Florida papers, and invited myself for a visit. Over a long weekend we devised "top of the stove" turkey dishes: Chinese turkey slivers, white meat turkey salad and turkey aspic. An 11- to 12-pound turkey yields a total of 5¾ pounds boneless meat, about 4 cups of dark meat and 6–7 cups white meat.

TOP OF THE STOVE TURKEY

18 cups water

2 cups sliced celery with leaves

1 onion peeled and stuck with a
    clove

3 sprigs fresh parsley

2–3 lettuce leaves

2 bay leaves

8 peppercorns

1 tablespoon salt

1 thawed turkey, 11–12 pounds

In a large kettle combine water, celery, onion, parsley, lettuce leaves, bay leaves, peppercorns and salt. Bring to the boiling point, then cover and simmer for about 45 minutes. Meantime, cut turkey up like a chicken, 2 legs and thighs, 2 wings, 2 half breasts. Use a long sharp knife to disjoint and a smaller one to remove breasts in one piece. Do not be afraid if some meat still adheres to the carcass; it will be recovered. Set aside one raw breast for Chinese turkey slivers, see p. 96. Reserve liver for other purposes.

Add the rest of the cut-up turkey, including the carcass and giblets, to the broth. Bring back to the boiling point, reduce to a simmer and cook for about 30 minutes. Remove other breast half, cool and use for turkey salad (see p. 96). Remove carcass and wings and let cool to be stripped. Cook legs and thighs for 15 minutes longer, till tender. Remove from broth to be used for turkey aspic (see p. 97). Let turkey parts cool enough to handle, then strip all the meat from bones. Keep white meat and dark meat separate. There will be about 4 cups dark meat and 4 cups white meat. Note: If there is no immediate use for the meat, wrap well and freeze. Strain broth—about 16 cups—and if there is no immediate use for it, freeze it.

BREAST OF TURKEY CHINESE STYLE

½ raw boneless breast of turkey   *3 tablespoons soy sauce*
from a 11½- to 12-   *2 pieces cracked ginger*
pound turkey   *1 cup flour*
⅓ cup lemon juice (3–4 lemons)   *Oil for shallow frying*

Cut turkey in strips from one quarter to one half inch in thickness. Add lemon juice, soy sauce and ginger. Mix lightly, then cover and marinate for 8 hours. Turn pieces twice.

Remove turkey from marinade, discard marinade. Pat turkey pieces dry with paper towels. Put flour in a bag and shake a few pieces at the time to coat strips. Arrange on a rack to let superfluous flour drop off.

Heat enough oil in a 9-inch frying pan to about one quarter inch. When oil is hot but not smoking cook the turkey pieces for a minute or two on each side, a few at a time. Put on paper towels to dry. Then cool and refrigerate until ready to serve.

6 SERVINGS

TURKEY SALAD

4 cups diced cooked turkey breast   *½ cup sour cream*
1 cup diced celery   *Drained grapefruit sections and*
1 tablespoon minced onion   *watercress, optional*
½ cup mayonnaise

Mix turkey meat and celery. Blend together mayonnaise and sour cream. Combine and chill. For a Florida touch garnish with drained grapefruit sections and watercress.

8 SERVINGS

TURKEY IN ASPIC

12 *cups turkey broth*
4 *cups coarsely chopped dark tur-*
   key meat
8 *envelopes plain gelatin*
½–¾ *cup vinegar, depending on*
   strength and flavor

1½ *cups chopped olives, pimien-*
   tos and mixed pickles in
   proportions to suit in-
   dividual taste
2 *sliced hard cooked eggs for*
   garnish
Slices of olives for garnish

Pour 6 cups of broth in a saucepan. Sprinkle gelatin on top and heat slowly, stirring constantly to dissolve gelatin. Add remaining 6 cups broth, add vinegar and taste. If needed, add more vinegar. Reserve ½ cup broth for garnish and keep at room temperature. Chill the remaining broth to egg white consistency (set in a bowl of ice if in a hurry).

Combine jellied broth, turkey meat and olive mixture. Divide between 2 6-cup loaf pans. Chill until firm. Unmold loaves on chilled platters. Dip sliced eggs and olives in reserved ½ cup broth and place on top of loaves. Chill to set. Serve with mayonnaise slightly thinned with sour cream and flavored with dried tarragon.

EACH LOAF, 6–8 SERVINGS

Note: If desired, cut the aspic recipe in half and use 2 cups of turkey meat for herring salad (see page 61).

ROAST BREAST OF TURKEY

This is a lazy way of roasting a frozen breast of turkey.

   1 *frozen breast of turkey* (3¼ *pounds*)
   8–10 *slices of bacon*
   Toothpicks

Defrost turkey breast thoroughly. Rinse with cold water, then pat dry. Arrange slices of bacon over breast, securing each slice on both ends with toothpicks.

Preheat oven to 325° F. Place turkey breast in a small roasting pan. Put in oven and roast for 1½ hours. Remove from oven, take off bacon slices. (Don't discard. Fry until crisp, crumble, and use in salad or for other purposes.) Chill completely before slicing.

WILL SERVE 8 FOR DINNER, 10–12 FOR BUFFET WITH OTHER MEATS

Note: Large breasts will roast at 325° F as follows:
       5–8 pounds, 2½–3½ hours
       8–10 pounds, 3½–4 hours

SALADS

FIFTY-FIFTY APPLE COLE SLAW

    1 pound fresh sauerkraut
    2 cups shredded cabbage
    2 tablespoons chopped nuts, any variety
    1 tart apple

DRESSING:

    1 cup apple juice, unsweetened   *½ teaspoon dry mustard*
    2 tablespoons flour   *½ teaspoon salt*
    2 egg yolks   *¼ teaspoon pepper*

Rinse sauerkraut well and press dry. Mix with shredded cabbage and chopped nuts. Prepare dressing by combining all ingredients and beating with a wire whisk. Over very low heat or a double boiler bring slowly to the boiling point, stirring constantly. When thickened, remove from fire and cool for a few minutes, then add to the cabbage mixture. Peel and core apple and shred into the cabbage salad, mixing in immediately to prevent discoloration. Chill and serve as any other cole slaw.

MAKES 1 QUART

CUCUMBER SALAD IN ZUCCHINI TROUGHS

1 zucchini, about 7 inches long and 2 inches thick
1 medium-sized cucumber
1 tablespoon salt

3 tablespoons sour cream
2 tablespoons fresh dill, chopped
½ teaspoon pepper

Scrub zucchini and drop into boiling salted water. After water returns to the boiling point, simmer for 1 minute. Remove and chill. When cooled cut in half through the middle, then trim off ends; cut in half neatly lengthwise and scoop out seeds (a grapefruit knife is quite handy). Chill. Peel cucumber, cut in half through middle, then halve each part. Scoop out seeds. Slice thinly into halfmoons like a celery stalk. Place in bowl and sprinkle with salt. Let stand for 1–2 hours. Drain and shake dry. Mix sour cream, pepper and fresh dill, beating with a fork or wire whisk; add to cucumbers. Fill zucchini troughs with cucumbers and garnish if desired with a strip of pimiento or dust with paprika.

4 SERVINGS

CHINESE CABBAGE SALAD

1 head of Chinese cabbage (about 2–3 pounds)
3 tablespoons dry mustard

3 tablespoons soy sauce
3 teaspoons cider vinegar
1 teaspoon salt

Trim off outer cabbage leaves and cut cabbage into 1-inch pieces from tip to stem. Drop cabbage leaf pieces into hot boiling water, enough to cover, and blanch for 1 minute. Drain well; then put in a bowl.

Mix mustard, soy sauce, vinegar and salt and pour over hot cabbage. Mix well. Chill before serving.

MAKES ABOUT 1 QUART

ZUCCHINI SALAD

8 small baby zucchinis (about 1½–2 pounds)
Salt
Water

DRESSING:

1 egg	*Juice of 2 lemons*
1 cup salad oil	*4–5 scallions, white part*
1 teaspoon salt	*1 teaspoon tomato paste*

Scrub zucchinis, trim off both ends, cover with water, add salt, and bring to the boiling point. Cook for 5–7 minutes at high heat. Drain and cool until ready to handle. Cut lengthwise into quarters, then cut each through the middle into pieces about 3 inches long. Do not chill but prepare the dressing: Put egg in blender and beat, add about ⅓ of the oil and beat, then slowly add the remaining oil, blending all the time. When thick, add salt, lemon juice and the cut-up scallions freed from all outer skins. Add tomato paste. Use part of this dressing to coat the still warm zucchinis and chill. Chill the remaining dressing and serve on the side.

8–10 SERVINGS

FRESH LIMA BEAN SALAD

2 packages frozen baby lima beans   1 teaspoon salt
    (10 ounces each)   1½ cups water
3 tablespoons minced instant
    onion

DRESSING:

4 tablespoons vegetable oil   ½ teaspoon salt
1 tablespoon tarragon vinegar   ¼ teaspoon pepper
Pinch of dry mustard

GARNISH:

½ can sliced baby tomatoes, drained

Put lima beans, onions, salt and water in a saucepan and boil until lima beans are just done, about 15 minutes. Drain through a fine sieve. Put in a bowl. Blend oil, vinegar, mustard, salt and pepper very well until cloudy, then pour over the hot lima bean mixture. Let stand for 20 minutes, then add drained tomatoes. Mix lightly and chill.

8–10 SERVINGS

GREEN BEAN SALAD

2 cans whole green beans (Blue   ¾ cup oil
    Lake variety, 16 ounces   3 tablespoons tarragon vinegar
    each)   1 teaspoon salt
1 tablespoon dry onion flakes   ½ teaspoon pepper
¼ teaspoon summer savory

Empty beans into a saucepan, add onion flakes and summer savory and simmer for 5 minutes. Drain and keep warm. Blend oil, vinegar, salt and pepper until cloudy, then pour over warm beans; toss to blend well. Chill before serving.

8–10 SERVINGS

FRESH ASPARAGUS SALAD

3–5 pounds fresh asparagus
1 tablespoon salt
Juice of 4 lemons
or

VINAIGRETTE:

½ cup oil	*1 teaspoon salt*
3 tablespoons lemon juice	*½ teaspoon pepper*
1 tablespoon chopped parsley	

GARNISH:

2 chopped hard-cooked egg whites
Pimiento strips

How many stalks of asparagus per person? That depends on the thickness of the stalks and "Of course, asparagus is my favorite food!" So it's up to the hostess. Try to find a produce stand that allows picking and choosing and select the thickness of stalk you prefer. Individual bunches of asparagus usually have stalks of fairly uniform thickness. (Don't be wary of asparagus stalks that look like fattened grass blades, they are of very good flavor.) For very thick stalks, allow 5–6 per serving; medium stalks about 7–8 and thinnish ones as many as 10 for a generous salad course. In any case, whatever size the stalks may be, cut off the tough ends. For a salad, try to make them of even length. Wash the cut-off pieces, cover them with water, add 1 tablespoon salt, press out 1 lemon (reserving the juice) and add the lemon shells to the cut-off stalks. Simmer for ¾–1 hour. Put the

SALADS   103

trimmed asparagus in water and let soak. After 15 minutes, test the water for sand particles. If there is sand, scrub the stalks, otherwise it is not necessary. Wrap the washed stalks in cheesecloth—all heads in one direction—and place them in a vessel that holds them easily. Press out 2 more lemons, reserving the juice, and add to the stalks. Strain the hot broth from the cut-offs over the asparagus. Add more water if needed to cover. Simmer for 15–20 minutes (or longer for very thick stalks). Test with a fork for doneness. Drain off some of the water but take care not to tip the pot at the side of the heads, they could be squashed by the weight. Lift the asparagus out with the cheesecloth and put on a platter. Remove cheesecloth and drain off any water. Pat dry with paper toweling. While still hot, pour the juice of the 4 lemons over the stalks. Repeatedly baste with the juice, then chill, basting every once in a while until ready to serve. Or beat together ½ cup oil and the 3 tablespoons lemon juice, add parsley, salt and pepper and pour over the hot stalks. Again, repeatedly baste with the liquid. Then chill. Just before serving sprinkle with the chopped eggs and garnish with the pimiento strips.

SMALL AVERAGE SERVING: 3 PORTIONS PER POUND.
BEST TO COUNT STALKS.

FRENCHY TOMATOES

4–5 large tomatoes   *1 teaspoon salt*
½ cup oil   *1 cup chopped parsley*
3 tablespoons lemon juice

Spear tomatoes at blossom end and hold into boiling water for 30–45 seconds. Blanch them, one at a time. Cool a bit, then peel (skin comes off easily). Cut into thick slices about ½–¾ inch. Arrange on a flat surface. Beat oil and lemon juice until cloudy, add salt and beat some more. Put in a bowl and add parsley. Spread this over the sliced tomatoes. Chill. Baste with any dressing that has seeped from the tomatoes while chilling. Use as a garnish or serve on lettuce leaves as a salad.

12–15 SLICES

LENTIL SALAD

6 cups water	*½ teaspoon salt*
2 bouillon cubes, beef or chicken	*1 cup lentils*
½ cup cider vinegar	

DRESSING:

3 tablespoons oil	*½ onion, sliced paper thin with*
1 tablespoon cider vinegar	*potato peeler (about ½*
1 teaspoon salt	*cup)*
½ teaspoon pepper	

Combine water, bouillon cubes, vinegar and salt and bring to the boiling point. Add lentils and cook for about 30–35 minutes until they are just soft. Drain. Combine oil, vinegar, salt and pepper and beat until well blended. Pour over hot lentils. Cool, then add paper thin onions. Mix well. Chill before serving.

6 SERVINGS

PICKLED RICE SALAD

1 can pickled beets (16 ounces)	*2 tablespoons vinegar*
½ cup converted rice	*1 apple*
½ teaspoon salt	

Drain beets and on the sieve coarsely chop the beets. Measure the beet liquid and add enough water to make 1½ cups. Add the ½ cup rice, salt and vinegar. Boil covered, until rice is done and cook un-covered for last 5 minutes. Peel and core apple and slice. Add to beets. Add rice to beets, taste for seasoning and if desired add a teaspoon or so more of vinegar. Cool and chill.

MAKES I QUART

GREEN NOODLE SALAD, IN TOMATO CUPS

½ package spinach noodles or macaroni (approximately 4 ounces, broken into 1-inch pieces)
1½ cups chopped onions
3 tablespoons vegetable oil
1 teaspoon salt
½ teaspoon pepper
2 tablespoons vinegar
3 tablespoons mayonnaise
6 tomatoes, scooped out and drained

Cook spinach noodle pieces in salted water according to directions on package until quite soft. In a frying pan combine onions and oil and slowly cook until onions are soft and begin to brown. (Start with a high flame, then reduce heat so as not to burn onions.) When onions are done, add vinegar, salt and pepper. Drain noodles and shake dry. While still hot, add onions to noodles and mix well. Let cool for 15 minutes, then add mayonnaise, blending it in well, spoon by spoon. Remove blossom end from tomatoes and scoop out seeds; turn upside down to drain. Fill with noodle mixture. Chill before serving.

6 SERVINGS

WHITE BEAN OR GARBANZO BEAN SALAD

2 cups canned white beans,
   Italian style, or
2 cups garbanzo beans (chick
   peas)
1 scallion, white part only,
   chopped

1 tablespoon chopped parsley
⅓ cup oil
1 tablespoon vinegar
1 teaspoon salt
½ teaspoon pepper

Place either white beans or garbanzo beans in a small saucepan and heat to just below the boiling point. Drain. Place in a serving bowl, add scallion and parsley. Beat together oil, vinegar, salt and pepper until cloudy, then pour over the warm beans. Mix and chill before serving.

6 SERVINGS

SPRING GARDEN POTATO SALAD

2 pounds all purpose potatoes

DRESSING:

1 cup chicken broth, canned or
   homemade
2 teaspoons dry mustard
2 tablespoons tarragon vinegar

2 teaspoons cornstarch
1 teaspoon salt
½ teaspoon pepper

GARNISH:

3 scallions, thinly sliced
10 radishes, coarsely chopped in the blender
2 tablespoons chopped parsley

Boil potatoes in the jacket until they are done (depends on size). Drain and cool enough to handle. Peel and slice thinly. While potatoes are cooking combine all dressing ingredients in a small saucepan; stir well.

Very slowly bring to the boiling point, stirring constantly. Cook until thickened to the consistency of heavy cream. Place a layer of sliced potatoes in a bowl; add a few spoons of hot dressing. Make sure to moisten all potato slices. Continue alternating layers of potatoes and the hot dressing until all is used up. Chill. Keep scallions, radishes and parsley cool and well covered. Just before serving, mix with potatoes.

MAKES I QUART, APPROXIMATELY

POTATO SALAD WITH BROTH AND BACON

2 *pounds potatoes*	½ *teaspoon dry mustard*
5 *rashers bacon*	½ *teaspoon pepper*
1 *cup canned beef bouillon*	2 *teaspoons cornstarch*
2 *tablespoons dehydrated minced*	2 *tablespoons vinegar*
onion	2 *tablespoons bacon drippings*

Boil potatoes in jackets. Put rashers of bacon in a pan and fry until crisp. Drain bacon on paper towels, reserving 2 tablespoons of the bacon drippings. Combine bouillon, dehydrated onion, mustard, pepper and the 2 teaspoons cornstarch. Stir to blend, then bring to the boiling point over low heat, stirring often. Add vinegar and bacon drippings. Leave in saucepan. When potatoes are done, cool them enough to handle, then peel and slice into a large bowl. Crumble bacon rashers over potatoes. Reheat dressing to the boiling point, then pour over the potatoes. Mix gently to distribute dressing evenly. Let cool, then cover and chill.

MAKES I QUART, APPROXIMATELY

WATERCRESS SALAD

2 *bunches watercress*	¼ *teaspoon pepper*
6 *tablespoons olive oil*	½ *teaspoon sugar*
1½ *tablespoons tarragon vinegar*	*Dry mustard*
⅛ *teaspoon thyme, dry*	½ *cup chopped walnuts*
½ *teaspoon salt*	*Juice of ½ lemon*

Wash watercress, toss dry and cut off hard stems. Chill. Combine olive oil, vinegar, thyme, salt and pepper and sugar. Beat with a fork. Dip moist fork into dry mustard and add whatever adheres to the dressing. Beat some more. Sprinkle walnuts with lemon juice and add to cress. When well chilled, beat dressing once more and pour over cress and nuts. Mix well.

6 SERVINGS

CAULIFLOWER VINAIGRETTE

Fresh Cauliflower

1 *fresh cauliflower, large*
½ *teaspoon nutmeg*
2 *teaspoons salt*

DRESSING:

¾ *cup oil*	2 *tablespoons capers, drained*
3 *tablespoons vinegar*	1 *tablespoon chopped sweet*
½ *cup chopped parsley*	*gherkins*
2 *tablespoons frozen chives*	

Trim end off cauliflower, remove leaves and cut into stem. Place head down in cold salted water for about 30 minutes. Bring enough water to the boiling point to cover cauliflower. Add nutmeg, salt and the cauliflower, head up, and simmer for about 20 minutes until stem is tender. Remove from water and drain. Combine oil and vinegar and beat until cloudy, then add parsley, chives, capers and gherkins. Pour over the hot cauliflower and set to chill. Baste with dressing while chilling. Leave head whole and use as a centerpiece for sliced cold meats.

6–8 SERVINGS

Frozen Cauliflower

> 2 boxes frozen cauliflowerets (10 ounces each)
> Salt and water as directed on package
> ½ teaspoon nutmeg

DRESSING:

> ½ cup oil
> 2 tablespoons vinegar
> ½ teaspoon dry mustard
> ½ teaspoon salt

COATING:

½ cup sour cream   2 teaspoons lemon juice
½ cup mayonnaise   4 shakes Worcestershire sauce
1 teaspoon dry mustard   ¼ teaspoon hot sauce, Red Devil
2 tablespoons tarragon vinegar

Cook cauliflowerets according to instructions on package, but add nutmeg. Drain. Combine all dressing ingredients and beat well. Pour over still warm cauliflowerets and toss to coat. Chill. Combine all ingredients listed under coating and beat well. Add just enough to coat well-chilled cauliflowerets and serve the rest on the side.

6–8 SERVINGS

GRAPES IN COTTAGE CHEESE

1 cup creamed cottage cheese (8 ounces)
½ cup milk
½ cup sour cream
½ cup mayonnaise
½ teaspoon salt
4 tablespoons lemon juice
½ cup water
2 packages plain gelatin
1 cup seedless grapes, cut in halves
1 cup dark grapes, cut in halves

In the blender combine cottage cheese, milk, sour cream, mayonnaise, salt and lemon juice; blend. Sprinkle the gelatin over the ½ cup water and heat gently, stirring constantly until gelatin is dissolved. Add to blender and mix. Pour in a bowl and chill. When cottage cheese mixture begins to thicken add the halved grapes, and pour the whole into a fancy 5-cup mold or divide between individual molds. Or pour into a ring mold and after unmolding, fill the center with more grapes. To unmold, loosen edges, set in warm water, count to ten, and reverse on a service platter.

6–8 SERVINGS

VEGETABLES IN BEER ASPIC

VEGETABLES: (any 3 of these)
1 package peas and carrots, frozen (10 ounces)
1 package baby lima beans, frozen
1 package very small onions, frozen
1 package cut green beans, frozen
1 package peas and onions, frozen
1 package cauliflower buds, frozen
1 package asparagus, frozen

Cook according to directions on package, drain and chill. Or use canned vegetables, drain and chill.

ASPIC:

1 cup chicken stock, homemade or canned
1½ cups beef bouillon
1 teaspoon sugar

1 cup light beer
2 envelopes plain gelatin
Salt and pepper to taste

Combine chicken and beef stock in a saucepan. Add sugar. Let simmer for 10 minutes. Put light beer in a bowl, sprinkle with gelatin and let stand for 5 minutes. Add beer gelatin to simmering stock, mix, remove from heat and let rest for 10 minutes. Taste for seasoning; this depends on broth used. Set a fancy mold on ice. Pour some of the gelatin mixture into it and let set. Arrange vegetables on top in a fancy pattern. Spoon over some more of the gelatin; let set. Alternate vegetables and gelatin liquid until all is used up. Chill to set overnight. To unmold, loosen edges, set in warm water, count to ten, then reverse on a service platter.

8–10 SERVINGS

BROCCOLI AND CAULIFLOWER SALAD MOLD

1 package frozen chopped broccoli (10 ounces)
1 package frozen cauliflower pieces (10 ounces)
2 cups beef bouillon (1 can)
½ teaspoon nutmeg

1 tablespoon vinegar
1 teaspoon salt
½ teaspoon pepper
2 envelopes plain gelatin
1 tablespoon vinegar

Cook the chopped broccoli until just soft in the bouillon to which the nutmeg, vinegar, salt and pepper have been added. Drain the liquid and pour over the cauliflower and cook this until just done. Drain and measure cooking liquid. Put enough cold water into a saucepan to bring liquid total to 2 cups. Over this cold water, sprinkle gelatin and heat gently to dissolve. Add to cooking liquid, add the remaining tablespoon vinegar and taste for seasoning. In a 4-cup mold arrange the cauliflower pieces, add a few spoonfuls of the gelatin liquid, then put the broccoli on top and again add some of the gelatin liquid. Then fill the mold with remaining liquid and chill overnight.

To unmold, set in warm water, count to ten and reverse on a service platter. Serve with mayonnaise or a green dressing.

8 SERVINGS

BEET AND ARTICHOKE SALAD PLATTER

1 can sliced beets (16 ounces)
1 1/2 tablespoons instant minced onion
2 tablespoons tarragon vinegar
1 tablespoon sugar
1 envelope plus 2 teaspoons plain gelatin
2 cans (7 ounces) chilled artichoke hearts, or 1 large

can in which there should be 8 artichoke hearts
Juice of 1 lemon
Water
1 1/2 teaspoons cornstarch
1 tablespoon Durkee Famous Sauce

Drain beets and chop coarsely (it can be done right in the strainer); put beets in a bowl. Measure the beet juice and add enough water to make 1 3/4 cups. Combine juice, onion, vinegar and sugar in a small saucepan and sprinkle the gelatin over it. Stir to mix well, then gently heat and simmer very lightly for about 5 minutes and pour over beets. Divide between 4 fancy or plain molds (about 1/2 cup each). Set aside and chill.

Drain artichokes; cut each in half, sprinkle with lemon juice and let stand for 10 minutes. Add enough water to the juice from the artichokes to make 3/4 cup. Add to this liquid the 1 1/2 teaspoons cornstarch and the 2 teaspoons gelatin. Over low heat bring slowly to the boiling point, stirring constantly. When the mixture is clear, remove from heat and add the tablespoon of Durkee Famous Sauce. Cool slightly.

Arrange artichoke hearts on a pie plate or other flat surface, cut side up. Spoon the liquid over the hearts. It will set almost immediately. Repeat once, then set aside to chill. If they are to be left overnight, cover lightly with plastic wrap or waxed paper.

Unmold beets on individual plates, then arrange 4 halves of artichoke hearts on each plate.

4 SERVINGS

CANNED ASPARAGUS SALAD

1–2 cans asparagus	*2 tablespoons vinegar (tarragon*
½ cup oil	*preferred)*
1 teaspoon salt	*2 teaspoons chopped parsley*
½ teaspoon pepper	*1 tablespoon capers, drained*

Stand the cans, opened from the "end" sides, in boiling water to heat through. Drain and place asparagus in a salad bowl or on a platter. Beat together oil and vinegar, add salt and pepper and beat some more. Add parsley and capers and pour over asparagus. Let stand for 1 hour, basting frequently. Chill.

Serve from the bowl or on lettuce leaves as individual portions. Garnish, if desired, with pimiento strips.

I CAN EQUALS 3 OR 4 SERVINGS

"ROSEBUD" BEET SALAD IN ASPIC

1 can sauerkraut juice (12-ounce can)

Water

2 envelopes plain gelatin

3 cans tiny beet balls (8¼ ounces each, also known as "rosebuds")

1 tablespoon drained horseradish, sharp

1 tablespoon grated onion

1 teaspoon salt

¼ teaspoon pepper

GARNISH:

Watercress for salad

Sour cream for dressing

To sauerkraut juice add enough water to make 2 cups. Pour 1 cup into a small saucepan, sprinkle gelatin over it and over low heat, stirring constantly, dissolve gelatin. Add second cup of sauerkraut juice. Drain beet balls and measure juice; there should be 1 cup, if not, add water. Combine beet juice and sauerkraut-gelatin juice, add horseradish, grated onion, salt and pepper, mix well and pour into a 6-cup ring mold. Chill until it begins to get creamy, then distribute beet balls evenly through the mold. Chill overnight.

To unmold, loosen edges, let sit in warm water, count to ten and reverse on a service platter. Put watercress in the middle and serve with plain sour cream or use any other salad dressing suitable for watercress. If desired, use julienne-cut beets and make up into individual molds.

8–10 SERVINGS

CUCUMBER SALAD

3 cucumbers
Salt and pepper to taste
1-cup container of plain yoghurt

1 tablespoon frozen chopped
chives
1 tablespoon chopped parsley

Peel cucumbers only if skin is tough and waxy. Slice very thin. Place in a bowl; cover with water. Add a few ice cubes and let stand for 1 hour. Drain very well, shaking and tossing. Place in a salad bowl. Sprinkle with salt and freshly ground pepper to taste. Beat yoghurt till liquid, pour over cucumbers, taste again for seasoning. Sprinkle with chives and parsley and chill before serving.

6–8 SERVINGS

SAUERKRAUT SALAD

2 pounds fresh sauerkraut
2 cups apple juice
½ cup oil
2 tablespoons vinegar
1 teaspoon salt

½ teaspoon pepper
1 tablespoon chopped onions
¼ clove garlic, minced
2 tablespoons chopped parsley

Rinse sauerkraut well and press dry. Put in a saucepan, add apple juice and cook for ½ hour. Drain sauerkraut; keep hot. Mix oil, vinegar, salt and pepper until cloudy and pour over warm sauerkraut. Add onions, garlic and parsley and toss until well blended. Chill before serving.

8–10 SERVINGS

BRAZILIAN SALAD

1 can hearts of palm (14 ounces)
1 can artichoke hearts (14 ounces)
1 large avocado (ripe)

Juice of 2 lemons
¾ cup mayonnaise
2 tablespoons heavy cream

Drain hearts of palm and artichokes. Cut hearts of palm into ¾-inch round pieces; cut artichokes in half. Place in bowl. Cut avocado in half, remove seed and with a melon ball cutter shape avocado balls, as many as possible. Add to hearts of palm and artichokes. Sprinkle with lemon juice and mix well to prevent discoloring. Scrape remaining pulp from avocado shells and mash with a fork. Add mayonnaise and cream, taste for seasoning. Beat well, then pour over the hearts of palm, artichoke and avocado balls. Carefully blend so as not to mash the avocado balls. Chill before serving on lettuce leaves.

8 SERVINGS

BROWN RICE SALAD WITH PINEAPPLE

This salad goes well with ham and sliced turkey. If desired, serve in half a pineapple shell.

1 cup brown rice, (3 cups cooked)
2 cups shredded fresh pineapple or unsweetened, canned crushed pineapple (see note)
1 cup shredded coconut or 3 ounces slivered almonds
Sour cream (about 8 ounces)

Cook rice; there should not be any liquid left. While still warm add shredded pineapple. Chill. Add coconut or almonds and just enough sour cream to coat well. Chill before serving.

MAKES 1 QUART

Note: If only sweetened crushed pineapple is available, drain and press syrup out. Then add ½ cup lemon juice.

TOMATOES DUBARRY

In the classic cuisine "Dubarry" spelled cauliflower. Why Mme. Dubarry should be connected with cauliflower is a secret, but she is.

8 medium to large tomatoes	*⅛ teaspoon nutmeg*
Salt	*2 tablespoons lemon juice*
2 boxes frozen cauliflower (10 ounces each)	*¾–1 cup mayonnaise*
	Chopped parsley

Cut a slice off the blossom end of the tomatoes. Scoop out seeds and pulp. Sprinkle inside with salt, stand upside down on a wire rack and drain. Cook cauliflower according to directions, but add nutmeg. Do not overcook; it should just be barely done. Drain and sprinkle with lemon juice while still hot. Chill. Chop very coarsely, just enough to break up the larger pieces. Add enough mayonnaise to blend, fill tomato shells with mixture. Coat top with mayonnaise. Chill. Just before serving sprinkle with parsley.

SWEET POTATO SALAD

The Cleveland Baking Powder Company of 81 and 83 Fulton Street, New York, published a small giveaway cookbook about 100 years ago in which there is a mention of "Conrad's Sweet Potato Salad." It calls for sweet potatoes, celery and French dressing. I embellished this idea and the result is the following:

1½ *pounds sweet potatoes (about*   1 *cup thinly sliced and then*
     3 *large)*   *chopped celery*
Juice of 4 limes   6 *ounces coarsely chopped*
2 *large apples*   *cashews or pecans*
                     1 *cup mayonnaise, approximately*

Cook sweet potatoes until soft; drain and cool enough to peel. Quarter lengthwise, then cut into cubes. Sprinkle with lime juice and chill. Peel, core and dice apples. Add to potatoes together with celery and nuts. Add enough mayonnaise to coat well. Chill before serving.

MAKES 1 QUART

WHITE RICE AND CORN SALAD

4 *large or* 6 *small ears of fresh*   2 *tablespoons minced green*
     corn   *peppers*
2 *cups cooked white rice*   *Juice of* 1 *lemon*
1 *small can pimientos (*2½   ½–¾ *cup mayonnaise*
     ounces)   1 *can flat anchovies*

Strip corn and drop into boiling salted water. Cook for 10–20 minutes depending on size. Cool, then cut the kernels off the cob over a bowl to catch the juices. Add cooked rice. Drain and chop pimientos and add, together with minced green peppers and lemon juice. Mix and chill. Add enough mayonnaise to bind. Place in a bowl, cover with more mayonnaise, then garnish with anchovy fillets, drained and patted dry. Chill before serving.

MAKES 1 QUART

MUSHROOM SALAD

1 pound mushrooms	*¼ cup oil*
2 cups water	*2 tablespoons lemon juice*
2 teaspoons salt	*½ teaspoon white pepper*
1 clove garlic	*Chopped parsley*
1 large onion	

Wash mushrooms and slice or quarter them; leave small ones whole. Place in a saucepan, add water, salt and garlic and bring to the boiling point. Reduce heat and simmer for 5 minutes. Drain, discard garlic. With a potato peeler sliver onion very fine, measure off 1 cup and discard remaining. Add onions to mushrooms and mix. Chill. Beat together oil and lemon juice, add white pepper. Chill. Add to chilled mushrooms, blend and garnish with chopped parsley.

MAKES ABOUT 3 CUPS

ONION AND WHITE TURNIP SALAD

3 large onions, cut up, about	*5 white turnips cut up, about*
2½ cups	*2 cups*
1 cup water	*Mayonnaise*
½ cup vinegar	*Chopped parsley*

Peel onions, cut into thick slices, then quarter each slice. Bring water and vinegar to the boiling point and drop onions into the liquid. Bring back to the boiling point, then drain and put into a bowl. Peel turnips, cut into thick slices, then dice. Add to warm onions. Mix and chill. When cool add just enough mayonnaise to bind. Add some chopped parsley if desired or use parsley just for garnish. Chill well for several hours.

MAKES ABOUT 1 QUART

OKRA AND PIMIENTO SALAD

2 packages of frozen okra (10 ounces each)
1 jar of pimientos, whole (7 ounces)

DRESSING:

½ cup watercress stems
½ cup fresh spinach leaves
3 sprigs parsley
*3 scallions, trimmed, white and
    green parts*

½ teaspoon dry tarragon
1 cup mayonnaise
Salt and pepper to taste

Cook okra according to instructions. Drain okra and pimientos. Cut pimiento shells into julienne strips and add to okra.

To make the dressing: Put watercress stems, spinach leaves, parsley and scallions into a small saucepan and pour a cup of boiling water over it. Bring back to the boiling point. Drain, press dry and add tarragon. Put mayonnaise in blender, gradually add dry greens and blend to chop. Taste for seasoning. Add dressing to the okra–pimiento mixture. Mix well. Chill before serving.

MAKES ABOUT 1 QUART

CRUNCHY PASTA SALAD

*2 cups pasta, such as elbow
    macaroni or shells, cooked
    al dente*
1 cup coarsely chopped celery
1½ cups chopped apples, peeled
1 carrot, coarsely grated
¼ green pepper, chopped fine

½ cup chopped pimientos
*½ grated onion (about 4 table-
    spoons)*
1 dill pickle
6 ounces salted peanuts
Mayonnaise

Combine cooked pasta, chopped celery, chopped apples, the grated carrot, the chopped green pepper, the chopped pimientos and the grated onion. Mix well. Peel the dill pickle, cut in half, remove seeds and chop coarsely. Add to other ingredients. Chop peanuts in the blender a few at a time and add. Mix all well, then add just enough mayonnaise to bind. Chill before serving.

MAKES 1 QUART

CURRIED BANANA SALAD

8 bananas
1 tablespoon curry powder
¼ cup grapefruit juice or orange juice

With fork mash 2 bananas until liquid and smooth. Add curry powder to juice and heat to the boiling point. Simmer for a few seconds. Cool, then add to mashed bananas. Mix. Into this sauce slice the remaining bananas about ¾ inch thick. Mix well to coat all slices. Chill for at least 3 hours. Serve on lettuce leaves in small portions.

8–10 SERVINGS

DRESSINGS FOR GREEN SALAD

FRENCH DRESSING

Basic

3 cups olive oil, or other salad oil   *2 teaspoons salt*
1 cup vinegar, wine, cider or   *½ teaspoon pepper*
tarragon

Variations: (To basic dressing, add:)

> *1 teaspoon paprika, or*
> *1 clove garlic, or*
> *¼ teaspoon dry mustard*

Combine all ingredients listed under basic dressing and shake well or use blender. Add any of the ingredients listed under variations. Keep in refrigerator.

MAKES 4 CUPS

RUSSIAN DRESSING

2 cups mayonnaise
6 tablespoons chili sauce
2 tablespoons minced pimientos

2 teaspoons minced chives (use frozen or use scallions)
2 teaspoons wine vinegar
Salt and pepper to taste

Combine all ingredients and blend well. This makes 2½ cups.

THOUSAND ISLAND DRESSING:
Use 1 cup Russian dressing (half of the ingredients listed above) and add ½ cup heavy cream, whipped.

"HOME STYLE" DRESSING

3 slices onion
½ cup tomato juice
½ cup salad oil
½ cup cider vinegar
1 teaspoon salt

1 teaspoon paprika
½ teaspoon pepper
½ cup sweet, thick condensed milk
1 clove garlic (optional)

Put onion slices in blender, add tomato juice, oil, vinegar, salt, paprika, and pepper. Blend until onion slices are puréed, then add thick

SALADS   123

condensed milk and blend well at high speed. Chill before using. If desired, add clove of garlic and let stay in dressing for 1 or 2 days, then remove. Shake before using.

MAKES ABOUT 2½ CUPS

ROQUEFORT DRESSING

2 ounces Roquefort cheese
1 tablespoon lemon juice
1 teaspoon tarragon vinegar
½ teaspoon salt

¼ teaspoon pepper
1 tablespoon olive oil
1 cup sour cream

Mash cheese with lemon juice and vinegar. Put in blender. Add salt and pepper, and oil. Blend. Add sour cream and blend some more. Chill before using.

MAKES 1½ CUPS

COTTAGE CHEESE DRESSING

1 egg
½ cup oil
2 tablespoons milk
1 cup cottage cheese
Juice of 1 lemon

2 teaspoons dry mustard
1 tablespoon vinegar
1 teaspoon dry tarragon
1 teaspoon salt
½ teaspoon pepper

In the blender, beat egg, gradually add oil and beat until thick. Add milk, cottage cheese and seasonings until well blended. Pour into a container and chill before using.

MAKES 2 CUPS

YOGHURT LEMON SAUCE

1 cup plain yoghurt
Juice of 1 lemon
Grated rind of 1 lemon
1 apple, peeled, cored and grated

½ teaspoon onion salt or 1 tea-
spoon grated onion
½ teaspoon salt

Mix all ingredients and chill before using.

MAKES 1½ CUPS

PARMESAN CHEESE DRESSING

1 egg
½ cup oil
1 teaspoon salt
½ teaspoon pepper

Juice of 1 lemon
½ cup heavy cream
½ cup Parmesan cheese, grated

In the blender beat egg, gradually add oil and blend until thickened. Add salt, pepper and lemon juice, and while blender is running add cream in a steady stream. Blend, then add cheese and blend until well mixed. Chill before using.

MAKES 1½ CUPS

DESSERTS

PEARS IN SHERRY

6 pears	*1 lemon, sliced*
2 cups sherry	*3 envelopes plain gelatin*
3 cups water	*Ginger marmalade*
¾ cup sugar	

Peel pears and with apple corer remove seeds from blossom end, leaving stems intact. Place pears in a saucepan without crowding. Add sherry, water, sugar and lemon slices. The liquid should cover the pears. Add more sherry and water if needed. Bring to a boil, then simmer until pears are soft, from 5–15 minutes, depending on ripeness of fruit. Remove pears to an 8-cup service dish and set aside to cool. Measure liquid (there should be 5 cups). Put 2 cups into a small saucepan, sprinkle with gelatin and, stirring constantly, heat gently until gelatin is dissolved. Add to other liquid. When pears are cool enough to handle, fill cavities with ginger marmalade. Set them upright in service dish, stems up. Add the gelatin liquid and carefully set to chill, *keeping pears upright.*

6 SERVINGS

BLUEBERRY MUFFINS

1 basket fresh blueberries	*½ pint (1 cup) heavy whipping*
1 cup milk, skim or whole	*cream*
2 envelopes plain gelatin	*3 tablespoons sugar*
4 tablespoons sugar	*1 teaspoon vanilla extract*

Rinse blueberries, pick them over and spread out on paper toweling to dry. Put milk in a small saucepan, sprinkle gelatin over it, add sugar. Stirring constantly, slowly bring to the boiling point. Put in a bowl, cool and chill until it has the consistency of raw egg white. Beat heavy cream until almost stiff; gradually add sugar and continue beating until very stiff. Add vanilla. When the gelatin mixture has reached the right consistency beat until fluffy, add to whipped cream and add the berries. Mix well and divide between 12 muffin tins lined with cupcake paper cups. Chill until set or overnight.

12 MUFFINS

PEACH SURPRISE

8 peach halves (canned)
1 box frozen strawberries (10
    ounces)
1 envelope plain gelatin
4 tartlet shells, or 4 "strawberry
    shortcake" sponge cake
    shells or 4 thick slices of
    pound cake

3 egg whites
½ cup sugar
¼ teaspoon cream of tartar
1½ tablespoons sugar for sprin-
    kling

Drain peach halves well, reserve some of the juice. Defrost strawberries and drain. Measure juice. Add enough peach juice to make 1 cup. Put ½ of this combined juice into a small saucepan, sprinkle with gelatin and, stirring constantly, heat gently until gelatin is dissolved. Combine with remaining juice and the drained strawberries. Chill. Arrange the tartlets, sponge cake shells or thick slices of pound cake on a cookie sheet. When using slices of pound cake make an indentation in the center. Place a peach half on top. When strawberry–gelatin mixture begins to set, fill the peach halves with the mixture. Place another peach half on top. Heat oven to 550° F. Beat egg whites until stiff, adding the ½ cup sugar gradually, spoon by spoon. Add cream of tartar. Coat the peaches with the meringue, pulling up some peaks. Sprinkle with the 1½ tablespoons sugar and put the coated peaches into the very hot oven. Bake until just beginning to show bits of brown. Remove and cool, then chill, or keep at room temperature if they are to be served the same day.

4 SERVINGS

SPRECKLED CHEESE CAKE

1 1/2 cups creamed cottage cheese
2 tablespoons melted butter
2 tablespoons flour
1/2 teaspoon salt
1/2 teaspoon vanilla extract
2 tablespoons heavy cream

2 medium-sized eggs
1/2 cup sugar
1 ounce grated semi-sweet chocolate
4 tablespoons grated nuts

1 prepared 8-inch graham cracker pie, or prepare your own graham cracker pie or use piecrust used for No Bake Lime Pie, page 136.

Heat oven to 300° F. Combine cottage cheese, melted butter, flour, salt, vanilla extract and heavy cream in the blender and blend at high speed until very smooth. In a bowl beat the whole eggs with the sugar until lemon colored and thick and sugar is dissolved. Add the contents of the blender to the eggs and mix well. Add grated chocolate and grated nuts and fill the 8-inch pie crust selected. Bake at 300° F for 45 minutes, then leave in the oven for another 35 minutes. *Do not open oven until the 35-minute cooling period is over or cake may fall.*

6–8 SERVINGS

SPOKED MELON

1 honeydew melon
1 can pineapple chunks (8 ounces)
1 can Mandarin orange slices (11 ounces)

1 basket fresh strawberries
2 tablespoons sugar
Orange juice
4 envelopes plain gelatin

Cut melon in halves lengthwise, remove seeds and cut each half into 4 or 5 long wedges about 1 inch wide in the center part. Cut off skin. Drain canned fruits; reserve liquid.

Wash, hull and halve strawberries, sprinkle with sugar and let stand. Measure juice drained from canned fruits and add enough orange juice to make 6½ cups. Put 1½ cups of these combined juices in a small saucepan, sprinkle with the 4 envelopes of plain gelatin, stir, let stand for a few minutes, then heat gently to dissolve gelatin. Add to other juices. Chill for about 30 minutes.

Set an 8-cup bowl or mold with rounded bottom in crushed ice. Combine drained canned fruits with strawberries. Put a few spoonfuls in bowl, add a few spoonfuls of gelatin juices. Arrange melon spokes upright against wall of bowl, using more fruit to hold them in place. Add more fruits and juices. Make sure melon spokes stand straight. Gradually fill in with more fruits and liquids until all are used up. Before setting aside to chill, push melon spokes slightly away from wall of bowl to allow gelatin liquid to spread all around and through the mold. Let set in the ice until ready to move to refrigerator. Allow to set at least 12 hours.

To unmold, loosen around the edges, then set bowl in a pan of warm water, or use sink filled with warm water, up to the rim, and reverse on a service platter. To serve, slice between the melon spokes.

8–10 SERVINGS

Note: If melon slices are too long for bowl or mold, cut them shorter and dice fruit. Add diced fruit to others.

MELON SURPRISE

½ cup rice	1 basket strawberries
1½ cups water	3 tablespoons sugar
½ teaspoon salt	1 cup heavy cream (½ pint)
1 cup white wine	4 tablespoons sugar
½ cup water	4 drops vanilla extract
2 envelopes gelatin	1 honeydew melon

COATING:

    ¾ cup water   *2 teaspoons cornstarch*
    1 tablespoon sugar   *1 envelope plain gelatin*
    Juice of 1 lime

Combine rice with water and salt and cook until soft but still grainy (about 15 minutes). Drain, add white wine. In a small saucepan sprinkle gelatin over the ½ cup water and heat gently while stirring to dissolve gelatin. Add to the rice mixture and set aside to chill, but do not allow to get firm.

Wash, hull and slice strawberries, but hold back about 6 or 9 berries for garnish. Sprinkle with the 3 tablespoons sugar. Whip the heavy cream, add sugar and vanilla extract, chill.

Peel melon, using a sharp knife. When hard peel is off use potato peeler to remove the inner softer skin. Cut a small slice from one end to make melon stand up. Then slice about 1½ inches down from the other end. Remove seeds through the opening. Reserve the cut-off slice. Chill. Combine gelatin–rice mixture with strawberries and whipped cream. Fill the melon with this mixture. Replace the cut-off slice. Chill. If there is any leftover filling place in individual molds or one larger one and chill.

To coat the whole melon and to decorate: In a small saucepan combine all ingredients listed under Coating and stir. Place over very low heat, stirring constantly, until the boiling point is reached and the liquid is clear. Cool for about 5 minutes. Remove melon from refrigerator and spoon some of the liquid over. With toothpicks fasten the reserved strawberries, either whole or half, depending on size, around the edge of the cut-off slice. Spoon some more coating over the strawberries to make sure they will stick after the toothpicks are removed just before serving. Repeat spooning coating over the melon. If the coating should get too thick, gently reheat, cool and coat.

Chill overnight. To serve, follow Jim Etro's advice and cut the melon right down the middle from top to bottom, then quarter each half. If there is any leftover filling serve some of it with each portion of melon.

8 SERVINGS

PECAN CREAM

1½ cups milk
1 envelope plain gelatin
3 tablespoons sugar
2 cups pecan meal or walnut meal
   or any finely ground nut
   such as hazel nuts or almonds

2 cups heavy cream
3 tablespoons sugar
1 cup pecan meal or any other nut
   meal

Put the 1½ cups milk into a quart saucepan, sprinkle gelatin over it and heat gently, stirring constantly to dissolve gelatin. Add sugar and the 2 cups nut meal. Let simmer for 5 minutes, then set aside to cool and chill. When this mixture is just beginning to set, beat the heavy cream, gradually adding the 3 tablespoons of sugar. When cream is stiff, add the 1 cup nut meal. Combine gelatin–nut mixture with whipped cream–nut mixture and put into a 6- to 8-cup service dish. If desired, garnish with nut halves.

8–10 SERVINGS

COFFEE KIRSCH

1½ cups water	½ cup milk
8 teaspoons instant coffee	4 ounces kirschwasser
4 tablespoons sugar	1½ pints heavy whipping cream
1 cup water	(3 small containers)
3 envelopes plain gelatin	5 tablespoons sugar

This is an old family favorite and can be made at noon to be ready for dinner, but it has to be an imported brand of kirschwasser to have the right flavor.

Heat 1½ cups water to the boiling point. In a bowl mix instant coffee and sugar and pour water over it. Stir to dissolve. Over 1 cup of water in a small saucepan sprinkle the 3 envelopes gelatin and heat gently, stirring constantly until gelatin is dissolved. Add the ½ cup milk and the 4 ounces kirschwasser. Add to the coffee solution. Chill until it begins to set, stirring the mixture occasionally to allow for even setting (if in a hurry, set over ice). When mixture has almost set to a consistency a bit heavier than raw egg white, beat cream, adding sugar gradually, until stiff. With the same beater, beat the coffee solution; when light and fluffy, combine whipped cream and coffee mixture. Pour into a service bowl that holds about 8 cups or more and chill until set. If desired, hold back some whipped cream and use for decoration or garnish with chocolate candy shaped like coffee beans.

8–10 SERVINGS

PUMPERNICKEL DESSERT

This is an old family favorite. It originated in the northern part of Europe where leftover black bread annoyed the thrifty housewives and heavy cream was plentiful. Use the darkest pumpernickel you can find; the best of course is the imported one, but any local variety will do just as well. Also, it is best to make this dessert the day before so the rum flavor can penetrate.

8 ounces pumpernickel bread	1 ½ pints heavy whipping cream
(usually 1 package)	1 cup sugar
1–1 ¼ cups rum	1 teaspoon vanilla extract
8 ounces semi-sweet chocolate	1 cup seedless raspberry jam

Crumble pumpernickel on baking sheet and dry in a slow oven, 250°–300° F. Put in a blender and grate fine. Put in a bowl and pour rum over it. The drier the bread the more rum it will soak up. Grate chocolate in a nut grater or Mouli cheese grater. Whip cream, gradually adding sugar and ending with vanilla extract.

In a deep (8-cup capacity) glass serving bowl, spread a layer of the whipped cream, sprinkle with pumpernickel crumbs and grated chocolate and dot with the jam. Cover with a layer of whipped cream, repeat the layer of pumpernickel, grated chocolate and jam. Cover again with whipped cream and repeat once more. Cover with whipped cream. Dot with dabs of jam and if there is any leftover chocolate use this for decoration, too. Cover lightly and chill overnight.

8–10 SERVINGS

FRUIT MACEDOINE

This is a fancy fruit salad, made up of assorted fresh fruits, filled in with canned and frozen fruits.

Suggested fruits are: peaches, pears, apricots, strawberries, raspberries, cherries, Persian or honeydew melon (do not use cantaloupe, the flavor is too strong) and grapes, cut in halves.

6–7 cups assorted fruits 1 envelope plain gelatin
Sugar to taste 1½ cups white wine
2 ounces kirschwasser 1 split of champagne, chilled

Drain all frozen or canned fruits. Sweeten to taste, pour over kirsch-wasser and marinate. Chill. In a small saucepan, place ½ cup of the wine and sprinkle with gelatin. Heat gently, stirring all the time, until gelatin has dissolved. Add remaining 1 cup wine and pour over the assorted fruits in a service bowl. Chill. Just before serving, stir the fruits and add chilled champagne.

10–12 SERVINGS

MANDARIN RICE

1 cup rice Orange juice
1 cup water 2 envelopes plain gelatin
2 cups milk 4 tablespoons sugar
½ teaspoon salt 1 cup heavy cream
3 cans Mandarin orange slices (11 ¼ cup sugar
ounces each) 1 teaspoon vanilla extract

Combine rice, water, milk and salt in a saucepan and cook until rice is done, but not mushy. Cool, then chill. Drain Mandarin oranges, measure the juice and add enough orange juice to make 1 cup. Put this juice into a saucepan, sprinkle with gelatin, add the 4 tablespoons sugar and heat gently, stirring constantly, until gelatin and sugar are dissolved. Combine with a little more juice, set aside to chill, but do not let set. Whip cream, gradually adding the ¼ cup sugar and the vanilla extract until stiff. Combine chilled rice, gelatin liquid, drained Mandarin orange slices and whipped cream and spoon into a fancy mold, or a 6-cup ring mold. Chill overnight. To unmold, stand in warm water, count to ten, then reverse on a service platter.

8 SERVINGS

AVOCADO CREAM

1 medium-sized ripe avocado	*2 egg whites*
1 cup milk	*1 tablespoon sugar*
5 tablespoons sugar	*¼ teaspoon cream of tartar*
1 envelope plain gelatin	*1 cup (½ pint) heavy cream*
Juice of 1 lime	*3 tablespoons sugar*

Scoop out the avocado flesh and put in a blender. Add ½ cup milk. Put the other ½ cup milk in a small saucepan, add sugar and sprinkle with gelatin. Heat gently, stirring constantly, until sugar and gelatin are dissolved. Cool to room temperature, then add to blender together with lime juice. Blend at high speed until puréed.

Beat egg whites, gradually adding sugar and cream of tartar until stiff. Add puréed avocado to egg whites, gradually folding it in.

Beat whipped cream until stiff, gradually adding sugar. Fold into avocado–egg white mixture. Pour into a serving dish and chill until set. Or fill individual serving dishes. If desired put in a fancy mold. Unmold by loosening edges and holding it in warm water, count to ten, then reverse onto a service platter.

6 SERVINGS

NO-BAKE 10-INCH PARTY LIME PIE

CRUST:

36 vanilla wafers (6 ounces), approximately 1½ cups, crushed
3 ounces butter (3 tablespoons)
1 ounce semi-sweet chocolate

Crush wafers in a plastic bag. Gently melt butter and chocolate in the same pan. Pour over crushed crackers and mix. Line a 10-inch pie pan with the crumb mixture, using the back of a tablespoon to press it down and up the sides of the plate. Chill.

FILLING:

½ cup lime juice	1 drop green food coloring
½ cup water	3 egg whites
1 envelope plain gelatin	½ cup sugar
½ cup sugar	½ teaspoon cream of tartar
3 egg yolks	

GARNISH:

Coarsely grated semi-sweet chocolate

In the top of a double boiler over boiling water combine lime juice and water and sprinkle with gelatin. Add sugar and heat gently, stirring constantly, until gelatin is dissolved. Add egg yolks one at a time, beating after each addition. Add food coloring. Cook until mixture thickens, stirring constantly. Remove from heat, pour into a bowl, and chill, or set in a pan of ice. When thickened to the consistency of raw egg white start beating until very fluffy. Beat egg whites until stiff, adding sugar and cream of tartar gradually. Combine the lime juice mixture and the egg whites and pile into the prepared crust. Sprinkle with grated chocolate and chill before serving.

8–10 SERVINGS

TEA CUSTARD

1 cup water	3 egg yolks
4 tablespoons loose tea leaves	¾ cup sugar
2 cups light cream (1 pint)	1½ tablespoons rum

Bring 1 cup water to the boiling point and pour over tea leaves. Let stand for 20 minutes. Strain into a 1½-quart saucepan, add light cream and egg yolks, beating after each addition. Add sugar. Over low heat, beating steadily, cook the mixture until it coats the spoon. Do not allow to boil. Add rum and fill individual serving glasses. Chill before serving.

4 to 6 SERVINGS

STRAIGHT UP APPLE CAKE

C R U S T :

3 cups flour	*3 raw egg yolks*
½ cup sugar	*3 sticks butter, melted*
2 hard-cooked egg yolks*	

F I L L I N G :

½ cup dark raisins	*10–12 tablespoons sugar mixed*
½ cup light raisins	*with 2 teaspoons cinna-*
¾ cup white wine	*mon*
7–8 medium-sized apples	

Combine flour and sugar; rub the hard-cooked egg yolks through a sieve and add. Mix, add raw egg yolks and stir. Melt the 3 sticks of butter and gradually add to the mixture. Gather together, then put on waxed paper and shape into a 2 X 3-inch-square block. Chill for

---

* This is a very old-fashioned but excellent method for making a light short dough. My mother learned it while in a famous cooking school; her teacher was a well-known pastry chef. To hard cook the egg yolks without cooking the whole egg, simply separate the eggs in the usual manner, reserving the whites for other purposes and leaving the yolk in the half shell. Wrap the egg yolk in the half shell in aluminum foil and put it upright in boiling water. Let simmer for 1 minute, then cover and let stand for 15–20 minutes in the hot water. Then peel and cool before rubbing through a sieve.
To hard cook egg whites, put them in aluminum foil and cook them the same way as the yolks. *The foil will be discolored, but that does not affect the egg whites.*

at least 3 hours, or overnight. Heat oven to 375° F. If chilled overnight, let the dough soften a bit. Cut into ¼–½-inch-thick slices and put on a 15½ X 10 X 1-inch baking sheet, reserving a few slices. Press the slices together, making an even layer. Cut the remaining slices in half and make the rim. Combine raisins in a bowl and pour wine over. (This may be done the day before when preparing the dough.) Peel and quarter apples, cut out core, and slice each quarter into either 3 or 4 slices lengthwise, about ½ inch thick in the middle. Stand these upright, with only a slight slant in 4 rows the whole length of the lined baking sheet. Sprinkle plumped raisins between the rows of apple slices and scatter a few over the top. Sprinkle with the cinnamon sugar, using more sugar if apples are of the sour variety; less if they are sweet. Bake for 1 hour and 15 minutes in a 375° F. oven. Apples should be soft. Remove from oven. Let stand at room temperature for at least 6 hours or overnight before cutting. If desired, serve with whipped cream.

MAKES ABOUT 16–20 PORTIONS

RICE TORTE

This was my mother's favorite dessert. It was the specialty of a small Konditorei in Berlin, Germany, when mother was a young girl around 1890. Jane Nickerson published the recipe first in the *New York Times* in 1953 and since then it has been printed in many publications.

FOR THE SHELL TO LINE A 9-INCH SPRING MOLD:

1 stick butter (¼ pound)	*1 raw egg yolk*
1½ cups flour	*1 hard-cooked egg yolk, rubbed*
¼ cup sugar	*through a sieve**

Melt butter over low heat. Combine flour, sugar, raw egg yolk and the cooked egg yolk rubbed through a sieve. Pour melted butter over

* See footnote on page 138.

mixture and work into a roll. Wrap in waxed paper and chill for about 1 hour.

Heat oven to 325° F. Cut the dough roll into slices and use to line the spring mold, pressing down with fingertips. Make a rim about 1½ inches high. Prick bottom with fork. Bake for about 40 minutes in the 325° F. oven until lightly browned.

FILLING:

2 baskets fresh strawberries
½ cup sugar
½ cup rice
1 cup plus 2 tablespoons water

½ envelope plain gelatin
½ cup water to moisten gelatin
1 tablespoon strawberry jam

GARNISH:

½ cup heavy cream
1 tablespoon sugar
2 drops vanilla extract

Wash and hull strawberries. Pick out and set aside about 12 very nice berries; slice the remaining and sprinkle with ½ cup sugar. Let stand at room temperature. Combine the rice and the cup of water, add 2 more tablespoons water and cook rice until soft but not mushy. Moisten the plain gelatin with ½ cup water and add to the cooked rice together with strawberry jam and any juice accumulated under the sliced, sugared strawberries. Mix well and let cool. Add sliced strawberries. Chill until the mixture begins to set, then pour into baked shell. Chill for at least 1 hour. Lift torte from spring mold by setting it on a can and pushing the rim of the mold down.

Whip heavy cream until quite stiff, add sugar and vanilla extract, and beat some more until stiff enough to be spooned into a pastry bag. Garnish top of torte in a lattice design and fill the lattice squares with the reserved whole strawberries.

8–10 SERVINGS

STRAWBERRY FLUFF PIE

CRUST:

1 cup flour	*1 hard-cooked egg yolk rubbed*
¾ stick butter (6 ounces)	*through a sieve**
1 raw egg yolk	*3 tablespoons sugar*

Put flour in a bowl. Set butter to melt over low heat. Add raw egg yolk, hard-cooked egg yolk rubbed through a sieve, and sugar to flour, pour melted butter over and gather into a ball. Shape into a round loaf and wrap in waxed paper. Chill for about 30–45 minutes. Heat oven to 325° F. Cut into slices and use to line an 8-inch pie plate. Prick all over and bake for 40–45 minutes until surface is slightly browned.

FILLING:

1 basket fresh strawberries	*1 egg white*
½ cup sugar	*2 tablespoons sugar*
Orange juice	*½ teaspoon cream of tartar*
1 envelope plain gelatin	

Wash and hull berries, cut them in half and sprinkle with sugar. Let stand at room temperature to gather juice, about 1 hour. Measure juice and add enough orange juice to make 1 cup.

Take ½ cup of this mixture, put into a saucepan, sprinkle with gelatin and heat gently, stirring constantly to dissolve gelatin. Combine with remaining ½ cup and chill to the consistency of raw egg white. Put over ice and beat until fluffy. Beat egg whites until stiff, adding sugar and cream of tartar spoon by spoon. Combine fluffy juice, egg whites and berries and pile into baked shell. Chill before serving.

6–8 SERVINGS

* See footnote on page 138.

CHOCOLATE NUT CAKES

5 egg whites

5 egg yolks

2 whole eggs

½ cup sugar

4 ounces finely grated nuts

2 ounces finely grated semi-sweet
   chocolate

½ teaspoon cinnamon

1½ tablespoons cornstarch

GLAZE:

2 ounces chocolate

4 tablespoons water

5 tablespoons confectionery sugar

Slivered almonds

Nuts and chocolate can be grated either with a nut grater or a Mouli cheese grater. (A blender is not suitable. It does not grate fine enough and tends to "ball" the particles together.) Heat oven to 350° F. Put 18 cupcake cups into 3-ounce muffin tins. Separate eggs. Add whole eggs to egg yolks; beat egg whites until very stiff, gradually adding half the sugar to whites. Use the same beater and beat the yolks and whole eggs until lemon colored. Add remaining sugar and beat until sugar is dissolved. Combine grated nuts, chocolate and cinnamon and cornstarch; mix well. Gradually add to egg yolks, then add half the egg whites, reverse and add to remaining egg whites. Fold in carefully. Divide between the lined muffin tins and bake for 35–40 minutes. Remove and let cool in the tins, then remove cakes and let stand at room temperature for about 2–3 hours. Glaze. In a small saucepan combine 2 ounces baking chocolate, 4 tablespoons water and 5 tablespoons confectionery sugar. Over low heat, stirring constantly, dissolve chocolate and cook until thickened. Using a pastry brush, glaze top of cupcakes. Put a few slivers of almonds on top. Let stand to dry overnight at room temperature.

18 CUPCAKES

MILKY APPLE SAUCE

8 ounces (1 cup) cottage cheese,   1½ cups apple sauce
      creamed   Sugar to taste
¼ cup port wine   2 ounces semi-sweet chocolate
Juice of ½ lemon

In the blender combine cottage cheese, port wine and lemon juice at high speed until smooth. Pour in a bowl, add apple sauce and blend. Taste for sweetness. Grate chocolate on the coarse side of a 4-sided household grater. Add some of it to the apple sauce mixture. Fill individual dishes and sprinkle with remaining grated chocolate. Chill before serving.

4–6 SERVINGS

POACHED APPLES WITH VANILLA SAUCE

6 medium apples   Red preserves: strawberry, rasp-
1½ cups water   berry or currant
1½ cups white wine   White wine
½ cup sugar   2 envelopes plain gelatin
                            Vanilla pudding (1 package)

Peel and core apples. Set in a saucepan without crowding and add water, white wine and sugar. Bring to the boiling point, then reduce heat and simmer for about 10 minutes, or until apples are just soft. Let cool in the liquid, then carefully transfer apples to a service dish. Fill the cavities with red preserves. Measure the poaching liquid and add enough white wine to make 3 cups. Use ½ cup of this liquid to dissolve gelatin in a small saucepan, stirring constantly while heating gently. Combine with remaining liquid and pour over filled apples. Chill to set. Prepare vanilla pudding according to instructions on

package for vanilla sauce (using more milk than for a pudding).
Chill and serve with apples.

6 SERVINGS

Note: Instead of white wine, apple juice may be used.

CHOCOLATE PUDDING

3 ounces unsweetened chocolate	*1 tablespoon instant coffee*
¼ cup water	*1½ ounces brandy*
4 tablespoons cornstarch	*1 cup heavy cream*
2 cups milk	*3 tablespoons sugar*
½ cup sugar	*½ teaspoon vanilla extract*
½ teaspoon salt	

In a quart saucepan combine chocolate and water, heat gently to dissolve chocolate. Combine the 4 tablespoons cornstarch with 4 tablespoons of the milk and blend. Add the remaining milk, sugar and salt to the chocolate and bring to the boiling point. Add blended cornstarch and instant coffee and cook, stirring constantly until thickened. Pour into a bowl and chill. Add brandy. Whip heavy cream until stiff, gradually adding sugar and vanilla extract. Combine with chocolate mix, pour into a service bowl or individual glasses and chill before serving. If desired, garnish with grated chocolate or miniature mints.

6–8 SERVINGS

CREAM OF WHEAT PUDDING

2 cups milk
¼ teaspoon salt
1 spiral of lemon rind
½ cup sugar
⅓ cup cream of wheat
3 eggs, separated

½ cup nut meal or finely chopped
   nuts, pecans, walnuts or
   almonds
Defrosted raspberries, strawberries, peaches, cherries

To the 2 cups milk add salt and lemon rind, cut off thinly with a potato peeler. Slowly bring the milk to the boiling point and let simmer a bit, then remove lemon peel. Add sugar, stir to dissolve, then slowly let cream of wheat run into the boiling milk. Cook until thickened. Remove from heat and let cool a bit. Add egg yolks one after the other, beating after each addition. Add nuts. Beat egg whites until very stiff and fold into cream of wheat mixture.

Either put into a 3- to 4-cup mold or divide between 4 to 6 individual molds. Rinse the molds with water before filling. Chill before unmolding. Serve with defrosted fruits with a fruit syrup or chocolate syrup.

BROWN BETTY WITH CHEESE

3–4 medium-sized apples
2 cups bread crumbs, dry
½ cup brown sugar

½ teaspoon ground cinnamon
¾ cup apple juice
1½ cups grated American cheese

TOPPING:

¼ cup dry bread crumbs
¼ cup margarine, melted

Heat oven to 325° F. Peel and core apples. Slice very thin. Put in a bowl and mix with bread crumbs, sugar and cinnamon. Put a layer of this in a 6-cup baking dish using about ⅓ of the total, then sprinkle with half the cheese. Spoon over some of the apple juice. Put another third of the apple mixture on top, follow with a layer of cheese and finally the last third of the apples. Add the remaining juice. Mix bread crumbs with melted margarine and spread over the top. Bake for 45 minutes. Chill. Serve with either fluid light cream or whipped heavy cream.

6–8 SERVINGS

FRUIT SALAD

FRESH FRUITS:

Cantaloupe *Grapefruit/orange sections*
Honeydew melon *Peaches*
Strawberries *Pears*
Grapes

FROZEN AND CANNED FRUITS:

Sliced peaches *Strawberries*
Sliced pears *Pineapple chunks*
Pitted cherries *Grapefruit/orange sections*

For each 6–8 cups of fruit, use 1 envelope of plain gelatin. Do not use fresh pineapple.

This salad is made with whatever fresh fruit is available and filled in with frozen or canned fruits. The greater the variety the better; therefore, only use small cans of the sliced fruits such as pears or peaches. I allow about 1 cup per person, which is ample. Cut the melons in half, remove seeds, then cut in strips about 1 inch thick in the middle. Cut into squares, then cut along the rind to loosen the precut squares. This is the fastest and most economical way to use melons. Melon balls are fine, but wasteful. When using fresh peaches or pears, make sure you have some citrus fruit already in the bowl before peeling and slicing, to prevent discoloration. Drain all frozen and canned fruits and collect the juices. Measure off 1½–2 cups, put half into a saucepan, sprinkle with gelatin, and heat gently to dissolve. Add to remaining juice and cool. Then pour over fruits in bowl. This will not make the salad an aspic, but will thicken the fruit juices to make the salad less runny.

SUGGESTIONS FOR GLORIFYING ICE CREAM DESSERTS

Note: Go easy, a teaspoon or two of the various liqueurs for each serving is ample.

Lemon sherbet: *diced bananas and Curaçao.*
Vanilla ice cream: *peach halves and blackberry brandy.*
Lime sherbet: *drained canned Mandarin oranges and apricot brandy.*
Strawberry ice cream: *drained canned or fresh halved grapes and brandy.*
Burnt-almond ice cream: *drained canned purple plums, pitted and quartered, and apricot brandy.*
Coffee ice cream: *whipped cream and rum, or crumbled macaroons and Curaçao.*
Peach ice cream: *chopped currant jelly and Curaçao.*
Sliced pineapple: *drained, spread with strawberry jam, topped with strawberry ice cream and brandy.*
Vanilla ice cream: *honey mixed with lemon juice and brandy.*
Apricot halves: *drained, filled with strawberry ice cream and apricot brandy.*

PALE FRUIT CAKE

Even in the summer a slice of fruit cake will dress up a simple dessert such as ice cream or stewed fruits. But try to find an honest fruit cake. The commercial variety has become darker and darker, presumably "richer," and is full of artificially colored, strange tasting glazed fruits. So I decided to bake my own. I took all the fruitcake recipes I could find, broke them down into solids and batter to get the proportions. I also decided to use nothing but pale fruit, just to be different. The first batch was made 2 years ago, and last year I had to bake 50 small cakes by popular request. The 6-inch disposable aluminum tins are ideal, as one of these is enough for 8 servings and they make such nice party favors for Thanksgiving and Christmas, to say nothing about taking them along as a hostess gift. As all fruitcakes they keep the year round in the refrigerator. All they may need is a bit of refreshing rum.

8 ounces candied citron	½ teaspoon salt
4 ounces candied pineapple	1½ sticks of butter at room temperature
4 ounces lemon peel	
6 ounces slivered blanched almonds	1 cup sugar
	¼ cup milk
15 ounces white raisins	7 egg yolks
½ cup flour	7 egg whites
1 teaspoon baking soda	½ teaspoon cream of tartar
1 cup cake flour	Rum or brandy
½ cup regular flour	

Butter generously 6 disposable aluminum tins, 6 inches long. Heat oven to 275° F. Chop coarsely citron, pineapple, lemon peel and slivered almonds. Put in a bowl, add raisins and the ½ cup of flour. Mix very well and set aside. Sift together baking soda, cake and regular flours. Set aside. With the same beater beat first egg whites, adding cream of tartar at the end, then cream together soft butter and ½ cup sugar until fluffy, gradually adding milk. Set aside. Again with the same beater beat egg yolks and ½ cup sugar until lemon colored.

Using a large pot, combine flours, butter and egg yolks, then add the fruits and mix well. Finally fold in the egg whites.

Divide between buttered pans and bake for 1–1½ hours.

Start testing with a cake tester after 1 hour. Let cool in the pans for 10 minutes, then turn out on a rack to cool.

Return the cakes to the cake pans and moisten with rum or brandy, about 1–2 tablespoons each. Put cakes in the refrigerator and repeat moistening with rum or brandy every 3–4 days in the beginning, then once a week. Make cakes about Thanksgiving to ripen by Christmas. After treating for 1 week, wrap them in aluminum foil.

Do not try to make a double batch, unless you have a very large pot. Rather repeat one batch after the first without washing bowls but using a clean beater.

FRUIT PYRAMID WITH LEMON COTTAGE CHEESE

1 pound cottage cheese, dry,
    Farmer cheese preferred
½ cup heavy cream
Grated rind of 1 lemon
Juice of 1 lemon
1 tablespoon sugar
6 slices from a small cantaloupe,
    without rind

6 slices fresh grapefruit without
    rind
6 slices canned pineapple, drained
6 slices oranges, fresh without
    rind
Strawberries, blueberries for
    garnish

Press cottage cheese through a sieve. Beat heavy cream until stiff. Add lemon rind and juice and sugar to cottage cheese, then fold in heavy cream. On 6 dessert plates arrange first the sliced cantaloupe, follow with a slice of grapefruit, a slice of pineapple and finally a slice of orange. Place a scoop of cottage cheese on top of orange slice. Chill before serving.

6 SERVINGS

SOUTHERN ORANGE NUTCAKE

1 orange	*¾ teaspoon cream of tartar*
2 cups pecan meal	*½ cup sugar*
1 cup dry bread crumbs, fine, sifted	*½ stick butter, melted*
	1½ cups water
9 medium eggs, separated	*1½ cups sugar*

Butter a pan 12½ x 9 x 2 very well. Heat oven to 350° F.

Grate the rind off the orange and set aside. Combine pecan meal and bread crumbs, add the grated orange peel and set aside. Beat egg whites until very firm, gradually adding cream of tartar. With the same beater whip egg yolks until lemon colored and stiff, gradually adding the ½ cup sugar. Combine beaten egg whites and yolks, adding the pecan-meal and bread-crumb mixture. Use a gentle folding motion. When all is well mixed, add the melted butter and gently fold in. Pour into prepared pan and bake for about 45 minutes; the top will be lightly browned and the cake shrunk away from the sides of the pan.

While cake is baking, combine the 1½ cups water with 1½ cups sugar, bring to the boiling point, then reduce heat and simmer for 10 minutes. Then squeeze the juice from the orange and add to the sugar solution. Cool to lukewarm. When cake is done remove pan from oven and let cake cool for about 15 minutes in the pan. Then carefully spoon the sugar-water-orange juice liquid over the cake. Let stand for a few hours to give the cake time to absorb liquid, then cut into squares.

8–10 SERVINGS

MY GRANDMOTHER'S APPLE CAKE

2 *large apples*	*1 cup flour*
Strawberry jam	*9 medium egg whites*
½ cup sugar	*1 teaspoon cream of tartar*
9 medium egg yolks	*1 9-inch springmold*

Heat oven to 325° F. Butter the springmold, then place a round of aluminum foil over the bottom and butter again. This is to prevent discoloration of apple slices. Peel and core apples. Cut them into rings and place into mold in one layer. Fill center of apple rings with strawberry jam.

Beat together sugar and egg yolks until thick and lemon colored. Add flour and mix. Beat egg whites until stiff gradually adding cream of tartar. First fold in ⅓ of egg whites into egg yolk mixture, then reverse and fold into egg whites. Pour dough over apples and bake for 45–50 minutes. Cool in the mold overnight. Place on a coffee tin, push rim down and turn cake upside down on a service plate. Take off bottom part, then peel off aluminum foil.

8 SERVINGS

CHOCOLATE STRAWBERRY SHORTCAKE

¾ cup pecan meal	*4 medium egg yolks*
1 cup sifted flour	*4 medium egg whites*
2 teaspoons baking powder	*½ teaspoon cream of tartar*
6 ounces sweet chocolate	*2 boxes fresh strawberries*
8 ounces butter at room tempera-	*¾ cup sugar*
ture (2 sticks)	*Whipped cream*
1 cup sugar	

1 9-inch springmold. Butter springmold and dust with flour. Set oven to 325° F. Mix together pecan meal, flour and baking powder. Set

aside. Melt chocolate over simmering water. Cream butter, add chocolate, sugar and egg yolks one after the other, beating all the time, until very thick.

Add the pecan meal–flour mixture to the egg–chocolate mixture. Blend. Beat egg whites, adding cream of tartar gradually, until stiff. Fold into the batter and pour into prepared springmold. Bake for 50–60 minutes, testing with a cake tester at the end. Cool in mold. Put on a coffee tin and drop rim. Cool overnight. Place on a service platter upside down, remove bottom part of mold, cut in half through the middle.

Wash and hull strawberries. Cut berries in half, sprinkle with sugar. Let stand at room temperature for at least 1 hour. Put strawberries and some juice on the bottom half, put the top half over strawberries and pour the rest of the strawberries on top. Serve with whipped cream.

8 SERVINGS

PINEAPPLE PAPAYA DESSERT

2 small pineapples
1 can papaya pieces
Sugar

Cut pineapples in half through the leaves. Then cut each again in half, making 8 pieces. Trim leaves and trim bottom end. Using a knife with a serrated edge cut off the hard core, then slice meat on the slant into thin slices. Finally cut along the bottom part to loosen slices. Cut 8 pieces of papaya into thin slices and insert them between the pineapple slices. Chill and serve with sugar on the side.

8 SERVINGS

Note: Any leftover papaya can be chopped and added to softened vanilla ice cream and then refrozen.

A PLAIN PUDDING

3 cups milk	*¾ cup strawberry jam*
1½ cups fine dry bread crumbs	*3 egg whites*
½ teaspoon salt	*1 teaspoon cream of tartar*
3 egg yolks	*½ cup sugar*
½ cup sugar	

Heat oven to 350° F. Heat milk to just below the boiling point. Add bread crumbs and salt and mix. Beat egg yolks with the ½ cup sugar until thick and lemon colored. Add to milk and crumbs. Pour into 1½-quart soufflé dish or glass baking casserole. Set in a pan of water and bake at 350° F. until set, about 1 hour. Remove from oven, cool a bit then spread top with strawberry jam. Raise oven to 400° F.

Beat egg whites until stiff, gradually adding cream of tartar and sugar. Spread the meringue over the jam and bake for 10 minutes until top is nicely browned. Chill before serving.

8 SERVINGS

FRUITS, RICE AND COTTAGE CHEESE DESSERT

1 cup regular rice	*2 cups cut-up fresh fruits or*
1 cup milk	*drained canned fruit salad*
1 cup water	*or other canned fruit*
3 tablespoons sugar	*½ cup chopped nuts*
1 cup cottage cheese	

Cook rice in milk and water until done, but just a bit grainy. Chill. Mix with cottage cheese and fruits, either fresh such as chopped apples, pears, bananas, fresh berries and grapes, or use fruits drained from canned fruit-cocktail mix or small cans of pineapple, grapes, diced pears, diced peaches. Add nuts, mix well. Press into a bowl and chill. Unmold on a platter, or divide between individual sherbet glasses.

8 SERVINGS

RICE AND CHESTNUT DESSERT

¾ cup regular rice
1 cup water
¾ cup milk
2 tablespoons sugar
1 can chestnut purée (1 pound, 1 ounce chestnut spread, imported)

½ cup heavy cream
¼ cup sugar
½ teaspoon vanilla extract
Grated chocolate

Combine rice, water, milk and the 2 tablespoons sugar in a pot and cook rice until done, but not mushy. Chill. Combine with chestnut purée. Beat heavy cream until stiff, gradually adding sugar and vanilla extract.

Combine with rice–chestnut mixture and chill. Pile high in a bowl and serve sprinkled with grated chocolate.

8 SERVINGS

CRANBERRY CUSTARD PIE

1 9-inch piecrust, unbaked, frozen or prepared otherwise
7 ounces cranberry–orange relish (½ of a 14-ounce jar)

3 medium eggs
1 cup Half & Half
1 tablespoon sugar

Preheat oven to 325° F. Prick piecrust and prebake for 10 minutes. Spread cranberry–orange relish over bottom. Beat eggs lightly, add

Half & Half and sugar and pour over relish. Bake for 45–50 minutes until custard is set. Chill before serving.

6–8 SERVINGS

A BIRTHDAY CAKE SO TO SPEAK
ESPECIALLY CREATED FOR BILL DAILY

SHELL:

Line a 9-inch springmold as described under Rice Torte page 139. Prepare as directed and let cool or chill overnight. Leave in springmold.

FILLING:

1 pound seedless grapes	*Water*
½ cup water	*2 envelopes plain gelatin*
1½ tablespoons plain gelatin	*1 cup heavy cream*
(1½ envelopes)	*2 tablespoons sugar*
1 cup white wine	*½ teaspoon vanilla extract*
2 boxes frozen strawberries, de-	*Commercial decorator set, red or*
frosted (10 ounces each)	*green*

Remove grapes from stems, wash grapes and let dry. Pat with paper towels if needed. Chill. Place ½ cup water in a small saucepan, sprinkle with the 1½ tablespoons gelatin and heat gently until gelatin is dissolved. Add wine and set in a bowl of ice to jell to egg white consistency. Put grapes into baked shell and pour wine gelatin over them. Chill to set.

Strain defrosted strawberries and measure juice. Add enough water to make 2 cups. From these 2 cups, put ½ cup into a small saucepan, sprinkle the 2 envelopes of gelatin over it and heat gently until gelatin is dissolved.

Put strawberries, juice and gelatin juice into the blender and purée. Pour into a bowl, set it on ice and chill until almost set. Then whip

DESSERTS   155

the heavy cream until stiff, gradually adding sugar and vanilla. Beat strawberry purée until fluffy, then add whipped cream. Before pouring this mousse into the springmold, lightly wipe the sides of the mold with a paper towel dipped in oil. Then pour in mousse over grapes and chill overnight.

To remove rim set cake on a coffee tin and push rim down. Commercial decorating cream holds very well on the mousse and so do candles. Serve like any torte.

8–10 SERVINGS

FARINA FLUFF

> 2 cups water
> Juice and rind of 1 lemon
> 1 cup sugar
> ⅓ cup farina

Combine water, lemon rind, juice and sugar and bring to the boiling point. Add farina and cook for 4–5 minutes, stirring constantly. Cool. Then pour into the mixing bowl of an electric mixer and beat for 20–25 minutes until very fluffy, snow white and the consistency of egg white meringue. Serve in sherbet glasses garnished with cherries or strawberries or other red fruit.

6 SERVINGS

ODDS AND ENDS

POACHED EGGS IN ASPIC

6 small eggs
About ½ teaspoon dry tarragon
    leaves
1 can chicken stock (13½
    ounces)

1 tablespoon tarragon vinegar
Water
2 envelopes plain gelatin

Heat oven to 375° F. Arrange 6 paper cupcake cups in a muffin tin. Sprinkle a few tarragon leaves into each cup. Measure chicken stock and add vinegar and enough water to make 2 cups. Place in a small saucepan, sprinkle gelatin over it and heat gently to the boiling point, stirring constantly. Put 2 tablespoons of this liquid into each paper cup. Drop an egg into each cup, then add enough chicken stock to fill. Bake for 15–20 minutes, depending on size of egg and softness desired. Remove from oven and spoon some more liquid over eggs. Chill for a few hours, then add some more liquid. Reserve any remaining liquid. Chill for a few hours or overnight. Reheat gelatin liquid and spoon some more over eggs. When set remove from tins and peel off soggy paper cups. Either coat with some more plain gelatin liquid or chill gelatin to the consistency of raw egg whites, then add 4 tablespoons of this to ½ cup mayonnaise and use to decorate the eggs.

6 SERVINGS

EGGS IN TOMATOES

4 tomatoes	*2 hard-cooked eggs*
2 teaspoons salt	*Mayonnaise*
½ teaspoon pepper	*1 tablespoon frozen chives*
¼ cup water	*Salt and pepper to taste*
1 envelope plain gelatin	

Cut a slice off tomatoes from the blossom end, about ⅔ down. Scoop out pulp and seeds. Put cut-off slices and pulp into a small saucepan and add salt, pepper and water. Simmer until very soft, then strain and press hard through a sieve. Measure and add enough water to make 1 cup. Sprinkle gelatin on top and heat gently, stirring constantly until gelatin is dissolved. Set aside to cool. Cut eggs in half through the middle and take out the yolks. Set the egg white halves into the scooped out tomatoes. Fill with the gelatin liquid and chill until set. Press the egg yolks through a sieve. Add just enough mayonnaise to make a soft paste; add chives and taste for seasoning. When tomato gelatin is set, cut each tomato in half from top to bottom. Put egg yolk mixture into a pastry bag and decorate each tomato half. This makes 8 portions. Or, if desired, leave tomatoes whole and decorate the top with the egg yolk mixture.

4 SERVINGS

MARINATED EGGS

Here are two versions, both of them time honored and once very popular. They make a good substitute for deviled eggs and can be kept ready to use for 2–3 weeks at least.

Eggs in Brine

12 eggs

Outer skins of yellow onions, as much as available but at least ½ cup, loosely packed

½ cup salt

Water to cover

Put eggs in saucepan, add the yellow skins (they will make the eggs marbled), salt and cover with water. Slowly bring to the boiling point, simmer for 1–2 minutes, then cover and let stand for 20 minutes. Drain water into a jar, it will be yellow. Let eggs cool enough to handle, then crack them all around and put into the yellow brine. Let stand for 3–4 days before using.

Eggs in Vinegar with Beet Juice

12 eggs

Water

½–¾ cup beet juice, drained from sliced canned beets

1½ cups vinegar

½ cup water

1½ tablespoons pickling spices

1 teaspoon salt

Hard cook eggs by covering them with water, bring to the boiling point, let simmer for 1–2 minutes, let stand for 20 minutes, then drain and run cold water over them. Peel and put in jars. Pour the beet juice over the eggs (use the sliced beets for other purposes). Combine vinegar, water, pickling spices and salt. Simmer for 10 minutes. Strain and pour over eggs and beet juice. Let stand for 5–7 days before using. The eggs will look brownish and be quite sharp in taste.

CHILI TOMATO CUBES

2 cups tomato juice
1 bottle chili sauce (12 ounces)
Juice of 1 lime

1 teaspoon *Red Devil sauce*
2 envelopes plain gelatin

In a saucepan combine tomato juice, chili sauce, lime juice and Red Devil sauce. Sprinkle with gelatin and slowly bring to the boiling point, stirring all the time, until gelatin is dissolved. Pour into a pan about 7 × 11 × 1½. Cool, then chill. When set, cut into cubes 1½–2 inches square and use as garnish or as a relish.

CUCUMBER MOUSSE

2 large or 3 small cucumbers
2 slices onion
1 tablespoon lemon juice
1 teaspoon salt
½ teaspoon pepper

About ¼ cup fresh dill leaves
½ cup water
2 envelopes plain gelatin
½ cup mayonnaise
½ cup heavy cream

Peel and seed cucumbers. Cut into pieces and put in blender together with onion, lemon juice, salt, pepper, and dill leaves. Blend at high speed until puréed. Put water into a small saucepan, sprinkle with gelatin and over low heat, stirring constantly, dissolve gelatin. Add to cucumber purée and blend once more. Pour into a bowl and chill. Do not let it set but add mayonnaise as soon as it is cold. Then let stand until beginning to set. Whip the ½ cup of heavy cream and fold into the congealing cucumber mixture. Divide between 6 or 8 small molds and chill until set. Unmold by loosening edges and holding in warm water. Use to decorate meat platters.

RADISH RELISH

2 bunches radishes

1/2 cup tarragon vinegar

2 teaspoons salt

1 tablespoon capers, drained

2 tablespoons olive oil

Wash and trim radishes. Drop a few in a blender and chop coarsely, then empty and add some more. Do not chop too fine. If desired grate them on the coarse side of a 4-sided household grater. Place in a bowl, add vinegar and salt and marinate for 2–3 hours. Drain very well. Add capers, mix and finally add olive oil and mix again. Chill before serving. It's on the sharp side.

MAKES 1–1 1/2 CUPS DEPENDING ON SIZE OF RADISH BUNCHES

SAGE ASPIC

This is fine to use with cold sliced turkey or chicken.

1/2 cup water

1 1/2 tablespoons ground sage

1 cup apple juice

1 envelope plain gelatin

1 drop yellow food coloring

Bring water to the boiling point and pour over sage in a small bowl. Let stand to steep for 15 minutes, then strain through a very fine sieve or use some cloth. In a small saucepan sprinkle 1/2 cup of apple juice with gelatin; gently heat, stirring constantly, until gelatin dissolves. Add remaining apple juice and the sage liquid. Add the drop of food coloring and fill two 1-cup molds or four 1/2-cup molds. Chill to set.

SMALL VEGETABLE ASPICS WHICH CAN BE USED
WHOLE OR CUT IN ROUNDS FOR GARNISH

Small cans of mushrooms, pieces   *Plain gelatin*
    and stems, julienne   *Lemon juice*
    carrots, asparagus pieces,   *Herbs such as summer savory,*
    green peas, green peas and   *basil, thyme, a pinch of*
    carrots, French-cut green   *ground nutmeg or ground*
    beans, lima beans   *ginger*

Drain cans and measure liquid. Leave vegetables in the cans. For each
1½ cups of liquid use 1 envelope of plain gelatin. Put liquids in a
saucepan, sprinkle with gelatin and add lemon juice and herbs to
taste. Add salt and pepper as needed, but usually the canned vegetables
contain enough salt. Heat the liquid, gently stirring all the time, to
dissolve gelatin. Divide liquids between the cans and stir with a fork
to distribute vegetables evenly. Chill until set. Loosen edges, hold
cans in warm water, count till ten and unmold. If there is any dif-
ficulty, open cans a bit from other closed end; the air will help to get
the aspics out. Use as a garnish, either whole small cylinders, or cut
them in wedges or rounds and arrange them overlapping around
sliced cold meats. If beets are used, either handle them separately or
have a pink aspic for all vegetables.

JELLIED SHERRY WINE

1½ cups water   *2 cups sherry*
2 envelopes of plain gelatin   *2 tablespoons orange marmalade*
½ cup sugar

Place water in saucepan, sprinkle with gelatin, add sugar and heat
gently, stirring constantly until gelatin and sugar are dissolved. Add
sherry and orange marmalade, divide between 8 small molds and chill

until set. Unmold by loosening edges and holding in warm water. Use as a garnish for cold meats.

KAY PEER'S SPECIAL CRANBERRY SAUCE

This is the best of all cranberry sauces. It keeps well, so it can be made ahead of the holiday season and is also very good on toasted English muffins.

> *1 pound fresh cranberries*
> *6 tablespoons undiluted frozen orange juice*
> *1 cup dry white wine*
> *2 cups sugar*

Wash berries. Use a 4- or 5-quart saucepan, as the mixture tends to foam up. Combine berries, orange juice, wine and sugar. Over low heat, stirring all the time, bring the mixture to the boiling point and make sure sugar is dissolved. Boil rapidly, uncovered, until berries pop open, about 7–10 minutes. Then cool and chill. This makes about 1 quart. (It's better to make 1 batch at a time so repeat, using the same pot for the next batch.) Fill in jars after cooling and keep refrigerated.

"RUMMY" APPLE SAUCE

This is another way to use up leftover egg whites.

> *1½ cups apple sauce*   *2 egg whites*
> *½ cup water*   *4 tablespoons sugar*
> *2 teaspoons plain gelatin*   *½ teaspoon cream of tartar*
> *2 tablespoons rum*

Chill apple sauce. Put the water in a saucepan, sprinkle with gelatin and heat gently, stirring constantly, until gelatin is dissolved. Add to apple sauce together with rum. When apple sauce is beginning to thicken, beat egg whites until stiff, gradually adding sugar and cream of tartar. Fold into apple sauce and chill again before serving.

6 SERVINGS

LEFTOVER EGG WHITE COOKIES

3 large or 4 medium egg whites
¾ cup sugar
½ teaspoon cream of tartar
¾ cup nut meal, either pecan or walnut

2 ounces semi-sweet chocolate, grated on a Mouli cheese grater
For the cookie sheets, 3–4 table-spoons nut meal

In a bowl, beat egg whites until stiff, gradually adding sugar, spoon by spoon, and cream of tartar. Fold nut meal and grated chocolate into egg whites. Heat oven to 325° F. Sprinkle 2 cookie sheets with nut meal. This will prevent the meringue cookies from sticking to the sheet. With two teaspoons set small heaps on the cookie sheets, about 36. Bake for about 30 minutes. Let cool on the sheet, then gently remove. Store in an airtight container after about 2 hours.

NEXT DAY ONION MUFFINS

4 tablespoons margarine
1 cup chopped onions, prefer-ably red onions
3 packages dry yeast
¼ cup lukewarm water
2 teaspoons sugar

2 sticks margarine (½ pound)
½ cup milk
2 eggs
4 cups flour
1 tablespoon salt

Melt 4 tablespoons margarine, add onions and sauté until soft but not brown. Set aside to cool. Sprinkle yeast over lukewarm water, add sugar and let stand. Melt 2 sticks margarine, but do not let brown.

Beat eggs, add milk and add the whole to the margarine. In a large bowl place 1 cup flour, add yeast solution, add more flour, then some of the egg–milk–margarine mixture and more flour until all is used up. Shape into a ball. Knead on a floured board until smooth and elastic about 5–10 minutes. Place in a large bowl or pot and add enough cold water to cover the doughball completely. Let stand for about 15–20 minutes until dough ball pops up. Remove from water, pat dry with toweling and again knead on a floured board, working in the 1 tablespoon of salt. Divide in half, then again into even quarters. Butter 2 muffin tins. Make 6 small balls out of each quarter and place in prepared muffin cups. Press down lightly and put about a teaspoon of the onions on top of each ball. Let stand until double in bulk in a draft-free spot. Preheat oven to 375° F. Bake for 30–40 minutes until a tester comes out clean. Remove from tins and cool, then store in a breadbox or a large stewpot with cover until next day —or later.

24 MUFFINS

TIPSY PRUNES, DATES AND APRICOTS

Dried pitted prunes	Pitted dates	Dried apricot halves
Port wine	Port wine	Sherry wine

Loosely pack prunes, dates and apricot halves in separate glass jars, and add the respective wines to cover. Let stand for 1 week–10 days at room temperature before using; after that they can be stored in the refrigerator. Allow space for the fruits to plump. Drain and reserve wine for use with the next batch. Do not wash fruits with water, if you feel they should be washed, use white wine. Apricots will get softer the longer they are kept in the wine. To be used with all cold meats, but especially with cold sliced beef. If dried peaches or pears are used instead of apricots, cut them in half or they will be too large after becoming "pleasingly plump."

DRINKS

COLD PUNCHES

Fruits and Wines

In general, the wines used are light, either white or red. Unless specified use 5–6 bottles of wine to 1 bottle of champagne or carbonated water, all well chilled. Champagne and carbonated water are best added just before serving. To sweeten, dissolve superfine sugar in boiling water, then chill before using. Do not try to "spike" these punches with a pony of brandy or whiskey. That way lies a beaut of a hangover.

STRAWBERRY OR RASPBERRY PUNCH

Use either fresh or frozen berries. For fresh strawberries use about ¼ cup superfine sugar for every basket of fruit. For the frozen, use only 1–2 tablespoons of superfine sugar.

2 baskets fresh strawberries or raspberries or	*Sugar*
	5 bottles light white wine
2 packages frozen strawberries or raspberries	*1 bottle (1 quart) carbonated soda water*

Place berries in a punch bowl and add sugar. Let stand for 1 hour and then add 1 bottle of wine. Chill. Chill also remaining wine and water. To serve, add wine and soda to berries and wine in punch bowl. Stir before filling glasses.

ABOUT 20 DRINKS

PINEAPPLE PUNCH

2 packages frozen pineapple chunks or	*3–5 bottles Moselle-type wine or California Riesling*
3 cups diced fresh pineapple, sweetened to taste	*1 ounce kirschwasser*
	1–2 bottles of champagne

Defrost pineapple chunks and cut them in quarters. Sprinkle fresh pineapple with sugar. Place either fruit in a bowl and cover with white wine. Let stand for 3 hours at room temperature. Chill remaining wine. To serve, rinse a 3-quart pitcher with the kirschwasser, discarding any liqueur that does not adhere to the walls of the pitcher. Put 1½ cups of the pineapple-wine marinade into the pitcher, fill with 2 bottles of white wine and 1 bottle of champagne. Serve. Keep pitcher on ice or in refrigerator. Refill as needed, keeping proportion of wine and champagne 2 to 1. Do not add ice cubes; they dilute the punch.

1 BOTTLE SERVES 4–5

CUCUMBER PUNCH

3 bottles of red wine, Bordeaux-type
1 cucumber
4 ounces Maraschino liqueur

Pour wine in punch bowl. Peel cucumber and add to wine. Let stand for 1½ hours. Remove cucumber, now soaked full of wine liquid and squeeze over a strainer to remove juices. Add liqueur and chill well before serving.

12–15 DRINKS

KALTE ENTE—COLD DUCK

1 lemon
1 tablespoon superfine sugar
1 ounce Curaçao liqueur

2 bottles of Moselle-type wine,
chilled
1 bottle of champagne

Peel lemon in such a manner that the cut peel is one continuous ribbon still attached to lemon. Prick the fruit with a fork and sprinkle with sugar. Pour Curaçao into a long narrow pitcher, swirl around to coat the sides, then pour out all liqueur that does not adhere. Now put lemon in pitcher and add 1 bottle of chilled Moselle wine. Place in refrigerator for 15 minutes, then add second bottle of chilled wine and the chilled champagne and serve. Do not add ice cubes but keep chilled by leaving in refrigerator or set in a bowl of ice.

10–12 DRINKS

A SPECIAL MIXTURE

4 oranges
1 glass white wine
Sugar water to taste (dissolve 1
    cup superfine sugar in ½
    cup water)

2 bottles red wine, Bordeaux-type
2 bottles white wine, Rhine wine-
    type
2 bottles champagne

Peel oranges, divide into sections and place in a small bowl. Add the
1 glass of white wine and let stand at room temperature for at least
6 hours. Prepare sugar water and chill. Strain liquid from orange sections into a punch bowl, add chilled wines and taste for sweetness,
adding sugar water as needed. Finally pour in champagne and serve.

12–15 DRINKS

PRICKED PEACHES

Fresh ripe peaches, unpeeled
1 bowl of superfine sugar
Moselle-type wine, chilled
Water goblets

Place a peach in a glass, let the guests prick the fruit with a fork,
spinning it around. Then let them add sugar, about 1–1½ teaspoons,
spin the fruit again and fill up with wine. The wine can be replenished
on the same fruit and finally the fruit is eaten.

STRAWBERRY WINE CUP

Bowl of fresh strawberries   *Moselle-type white wine, chilled*
Bowl of superfine sugar   *Champagne, chilled*
Water goblets

Have the guest place a few strawberries in the glass, pass the sugar, about 1–1½ teaspoons per glass, mix sugar and berries, squashing berries a bit. Fill glass half with Moselle and then fill up with champagne.

HONEY LEMONADE

1 cup honey   *5 cups water*
1½ cups water   *4 ounces vodka or gin*
Juice of 4 lemons

Combine honey and 1½ cups water in a small saucepan and heat until honey and water have combined. Put into a pitcher, add lemon juice and 5 cups water and chill. Add vodka and serve in Old Fashioned glasses over ice cubes. Garnish with lemon slices.

6–8 DRINKS

BLACK VELVET

1 bottle champagne
½–1 pint heavy stout

Chill both lightly and mix in a pitcher or in individual glasses. A good bedtime mixture.

5–6 DRINKS

ICED COFFEE EXTRAORDINAIRE

6 cups hot coffee, freshly made
4 sticks cinnamon
¾ cup heavy cream
Superfine sugar to taste

To the freshly made hot coffee in a glass carafe, add the 4 sticks cinnamon. Let stand for at least 1 hour at room temperature. Remove cinnamon sticks, add cream and sugar to taste and chill. Serve in highball glasses over ice cubes.

6–8 DRINKS

MINTED CHOCOLATE

12 tablespoons chocolate syrup (see page 172)
6 cups milk
6 drops peppermint extract (alcohol and oil of peppermint)
Whipped cream

Dilute chocolate syrup with one cup of milk, beat well, then add remaining milk. Add peppermint and whip some more. Chill. Pour into 6 glasses and top with whipped cream.

6 DRINKS

A CHOCOLATE SYRUP
FOR COLD DRINKS

Many years ago a South American friend gave me this recipe. It has one great advantage over commercial chocolate syrups: it is not too sweet.

1 cup cocoa	*3 tablespoons butter*
1 cup water	*1 egg*
1 cup sugar	

Mix together cocoa, water and sugar. Over low heat gradually bring to the boiling point, stirring constantly. Remove from heat, beat in butter, then add egg. Beat well, then return to low heat, continue stirring, and bring back to the boiling point. The mixture will thicken. When the boiling point is reached remove from heat, cool, then put in a pint jar. Will keep in the refrigerator for several weeks.

MAKES ABOUT 2 CUPS

ICED MOCHA

½ cup strong coffee	*½ cup milk*
1 tablespoon chocolate syrup (see above)	*1 teaspoon sugar*
	Small scoop of vanilla ice cream

Combine coffee and syrup and stir well to dissolve. Add milk and sugar; stir some more. Chill. Just before serving top with small scoop of ice cream.

1 SERVING

GINGERED ICE TEA

1 tablespoon tea leaves
1 teaspoon powdered ginger
3 cups water

1 cup orange juice
1 cup grapefruit juice
Sprigs of mint or orange slices

Combine tea leaves and ginger in a pitcher or saucepan. Bring water to the boiling point and pour over tea leaves. Let stand for 15 minutes, then strain and chill. Combine with chilled orange and grapefruit juice and pour over ice cubes in a highball glass. Garnish with mint or orange slices.

ABOUT 8 DRINKS

THE LONDON SANGRIA
A special recipe of Michael Rhode

1 apple
1 orange
1 small cucumber
1 lemon

2 bottles of wine, either red or
white
2 quarts lemon-lime soda
Sprigs of fresh mint

Peel, core and slice apple. Slice orange, peel cucumber, cut in half and remove seeds, then cut in pieces. Trim lemon, then slice. Put all in a punch bowl and pour wine over all, stir. Chill for a few hours. Just before serving pour in lemon-lime soda. Serve garnished with fresh mint.

6–8 DRINKS

WARREN KINSMAN'S BLOODY MARY

18 ounces V-8 Juice
12 ounces beef bouillon (no gelatin added)

Mix together and chill. This can be prepared the night before. To serve, pour over ice cubes as much vodka as desired for each drink, then add V-8 mixture and garnish with a wedge of lime. Do not use too much ice. No other spices are needed.

8 DRINKS

CLARET CUP

According to the *Bartenders' Guide* of 1862, the following Claret Cup "is a delicious summer beverage for evening parties."

To a bottle of "thin" claret add

2 cups water, cold
1 tablespoon finely powdered, superfine sugar
⅓ teaspoon each of powdered cinnamon, cloves and allspice, mixed
together
½ lemon

Mix all well together then add half the thin rind of a small lemon (use a potato peeler to cut the lemon rind). For modern use, reduce water and add ice cubes.

6–8 DRINKS

RED WINE AND GINGER ALE

> *1 quart ginger ale*
> *1 pint red wine*
> *Ice cubes*
> *½ cantaloupe*

In a pitcher combine ginger ale and wine. Chill. Dice cantaloupe or use a melon ball cutter. Just before serving add ice cubes and garnish with melon pieces.

6–8 DRINKS

APPLE PUNCH

> *4 apples*   *1 bottle Moselle-type wine*
> *2 lemons*   *1 bottle Rhine wine*
> *1 cup sugar*   *1 quart soda water*

Peel and core apples. Slice very thin. Put in a bowl. With a potato peeler cut off the rind of the lemons and add to apples. Add sugar. Mix. Pour over Moselle-type wine. Mix and chill overnight. Just before serving add chilled Rhine wine and soda water. Serve over ice cubes.

8–10 DRINKS

A HEAVENLY DRINK

2 quarts milk
4 ounces kirschwasser or cherry brandy
1 package frozen strawberries or raspberries, defrosted (10 ounces)
1 can crushed pineapple (6–8 ounces)

To milk in a bowl add the kirschwasser or cherry brandy. Put fruits in the blender and mash. Add to milk. Chill for at least 4 hours. Strain and serve over ice cubes.

ABOUT 6 DRINKS

THE SPOFFORD FIZZ
As concocted by Michael Rhode

"When you have Eggs Benedict for brunch, start with a Fizz, the egg whites from the Hollandaise, they just can't go to waste," was Mike's verdict. There were eleven of us in the Victorian cottage by the lake and the gourmet council had decided on Eggs Benedict for brunch. When everything was ready for final cooking there were about 3 cups of egg whites, left over from the Hollandaise. (Not to mention the fact that the night before the lobsters were served with Hollandaise instead of drawn butter. That left another batch of egg whites.) So here it is:

2 egg whites
1 cup grapefruit juice, unsweetened
2 teaspoons sugar
3–4 ounces vodka or gin

Put egg whites in blender and beat until quite foamy. Add grapefruit juice and sugar and blend. Finally add vodka or gin. Blend again. Serve over ice cubes in an Old Fashioned glass, right away.

MAKES 3–4 DRINKS

CRÈME DE MENTHE SODA

1 pint fruit sherbet, orange, lemon, lime
4 ounces crème de menthe, white
Soda, chilled

Let sherbet or fruit ice get soft, then add liqueur. Blend. Refreeze, but check while freezing and blend some more. Put a small scoop of the sherbet or fruit ice in an Old Fashioned glass and fill up with soda. Serve with a straw. Makes a simple dessert after lunch or brunch.

ABOUT 4–5 DRINKS

ED COTA'S CAROLINA SPECIAL

1 can frozen orange juice (6 ounces)
2 cans light rum (12 ounces)
½ can Grand Marnier (3 ounces)
Club soda

Combine orange juice, rum and Grand Marnier in a pitcher. Stir well. Pour about 3 ounces of this mixture into a tall glass, add ice cubes, then fill up with soda.

ABOUT 7 DRINKS

CRANBERRY PUNCH

2 cups water
1 cup cranberry juice
1 cup frozen orange juice
½ cup frozen lemon juice

4 tablespoons sugar
1 can cranberry jelly, chilled (16 ounces)
Carbonated water

Combine water, cranberry juice, orange and lemon juice. Add sugar and stir until dissolved. Chill.

Remove chilled cranberry jelly from can and cut into cubes. Keep chilled. Pour about ½ cup of juice into a glass, add ice cubes and fill up with carbonated water. Garnish with the cranberry jelly cubes. Unmold by dipping in warm water and reverse on a service platter.

8 SERVINGS

INDEX

Irma Rhode, born and educated in Berlin, has lived in America for forty years. A resident of New York City, she has worked or cooked or written or vacationed in most of the states of the union. In addition to her food careers, she has also been a chemist in the ceramics industry.